CREWEL EMBROIDERY

Erica Wilson

rewel

mbroidery

Illustrated with drawings by
VLADIMIR KAGAN

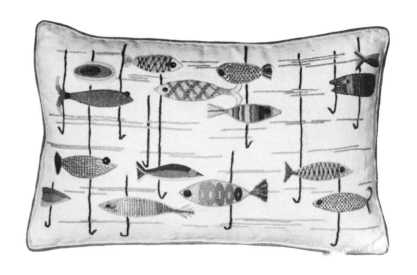

AND WITH PHOTOGRAPHS

CHARLES SCRIBNER'S SONS *New York*

Photographs on title page spread:

Curtain from the Abigail Pett bed, late 17th century. Victoria and Albert Museum.

Each fish on the pillow is worked in a different stitch. Designed by the author and worked by Mrs. Eugene Geddes.

Contents

Detail from the Abigail Pett bed.

This Booke some cunning workes doth teach
Too hard for some capacities to reach.
So for weake learners other workes here be
As plain and easy as A B C !
Thus skillful or unskillful each may take
This booke and of it each good use may make
All sorts of workes almost that can be nam'd
Here are directions how they may be fram'd.

The Needle's Excellency written by
John Taylor, the Water Poet, for
James Boler, published 1640

As Principal of the Royal School of Needlework where Miss Wilson gained the School's Diploma in Embroidery and Design, and subsequently was employed by the School as an Instructress, it gives me the greatest pleasure to write an appreciation of the book which she has written on Crewel Work. The writing of a successful book on such a subject requires, on the part of the author, an intense interest and a wide knowledge of her subject, to say nothing of a lucid style and a power of exposition. These qualities are, in my view, very apparent in the book which Erica Wilson has produced.

The words "Crewel Work" cover a very wide field. Miss Wilson has devoted a most interesting and instructive section to the history of this embroidery and I feel sure that this will appeal to all embroidery lovers. In the book are listed some "sixty-odd" stitches which are employed in the particular type of embroidery of which she writes. These, with their variations, would, in my view, cover any "piece" or project of crewel work, large or small. The stitches are carefully listed and described, and their method of working is as carefully given. The veriest beginner should find no difficulty in learning from these careful notes, how to work and to employ these varied stitches. The details of planning the design, choosing and preparing the frame, materials, *etc.*, should be of invaluable assistance to the novice, and indeed a guide to the more advanced worker.

Color, as Miss Wilson points out, is most important and yet the most difficult thing for an amateur to use. Her aids to the choice of color are most practical and should be of help to many embroiderers.

Since Erica Wilson has, on many occasions, given credit to the Royal School of Needlework for her training as an embroideress, I hope that it would not be amiss for me to say that that Institution endeavours to instill into its students the ideals of craftsmanship and a desire to "learn more." Miss Wilson has indeed profited by her training and I commend this book to embroidery lovers as a text book for all practitioners and as an encouragement to pursue the study of this most fascinating art.

Grace Hamilton-King
PRINCIPAL
ROYAL SCHOOL OF NEEDLEWORK

Introduction

What is Crewel Work? The answer is simple. It is embroidery on practically any fabric in wool: a firm, two-ply variety known as "crewel" which really gives the needlework its name. With these quite limited means, and a battery of stitches at her command, the embroiderer today will find the possibilities for individual creation innumerable. Since the background is complete before the stitching is begun, crewel work is quick – in keeping with today's pace of living. But more important, the time can be as gaily spent producing a bed-spread as an eye-glass case, for the great variations possible in design, and the changing effect of color and stitch, make the work all-absorbing.

Soon after man began to clothe himself, he looked for means of decorating and embellishing his garments. Evidence of early embroidery, e.g. stitches used for pure decoration, not utility, has been found on fragments of cloth and leather, and depicted on primitive sculptures and paintings. One of the earliest "stitches" was a twining stitch incorporated into the weaving, which was probably done with the fingers while the fabric was on the loom. Much later, embroidery was extensively used for religious purposes, and during the thirteenth century in England the most beautiful church vestments were embroidered with a special couching stitch which completely covered the fabric. These things were done with a needle made either of bone, wood, or ivory. But during the sixteenth century that great event took place – the invention of the steel needle, and England became the center for its manufacture. The period was one of great opulence, and never before had furniture and clothing been so richly decorated. The bed was one of the most valued items in the household, sometimes being large enough to sleep sixteen people. Laws had to be passed to prevent extravagant dressing, and embroidery was everywhere. This was the century when Mary Queen of Scots, when asked how she passed her time within, replied that ". . . all day she wrought with her Nydill, and that the diversitye of the colours made the Worke seem lesse tedious, and contynued so long at it till veray Payn made hir to give over." For the first time in England embroidery had turned from the church to be used

Painted cotton hanging or
Palampore.

Introduction

domestically. This is when Crewel Work, as we know it today, began. An exact date is impossible to establish, for it took one hundred years for the idea to crystallize, but during the sixteenth century Queen Elizabeth granted a charter to London merchants to trade with India. The East India Company began importing the printed or painted cotton hangings known as "palampores" and by the seventeenth century "Jacobean" embroidery as it was later called, had become high fashion. These palampores were probably Indian interpretations of English designs, sent out by the East India Company. Since the English artists were in their turn inspired by the fashion for Chinoiserie, the printed calico hangings were the outgrowth of a pot-pourri of cultural influences. At any rate, these printed cotton Tree of Life designs must have caught the fancy of the ladies who sat all winter long embroidering in their libraries. And they certainly were fascinating – a glorious array of exotic fruits and flowers, growing with naïve disregard for realism from a single stem, their branches filled with wild birds and animals, springing from the rounded hills of some far-away imaginary land. Within the conventions of the stylized pattern imagination could roam through groves of pomegranate trees, mountains peopled with strange elephants, leopards, even an occasional pagoda. If the whole effect seemed a little too exotic, then the embroideress might substitute an English deer, some strawberry plants, or perhaps an oak tree and acorns.

Owing to the difficulty of spinning a strong enough cotton in England, the material generally used for wool embroidery was a twill weave of cotton with a linen warp. The early English meaning of the word twill is simply "two threads," but later came the present meaning which describes material so woven that it has diagonal parallel ridges. This weave makes the material very strong and firm. Sometimes a twilled cotton was made with a nap, having almost the effect of plush. In many early crewel pieces this brushed velvety surface has worn flat leaving only the twill exposed, but by looking carefully under the stitching one can see that it originally was there. This type of twill was known as fustian – but names of materials were often altered with changing fashions, so

Curtains in the Wayside Inn, Sudbury, Massachusetts, designed and embroidered as part of the restorations; worked by pupils of the author from a design in the Cooper Union Museum.

Trumeau worked in silk and fine wool on antique satin

fustian may also have been used to describe other fabrics such as corduroy. The wool used for the embroidery was a tightly twisted worsted – so called because the town of Worcester was one of the main places for its manufacture. Nothing is known of how the word Crewel came into existence, except that it probably originated in the fifteenth century.

Many of the designs were monochromatic, relying for their effect on the "powdering" of the stitches, but often patterns were embroidered with many colors, such as butter yellows, warm earth reds, blues, and bright greens. It is a popular misconception that these Jacobean embroideries were done in muted colors. Though some of them may have faded, in fact the wools were originally brilliant and vivid, as is evidenced by those areas which have been spared exposure to years of light.

The bed was at first the most usual article of furniture to be decorated with Crewel Work. According to Hampton Court records Cardinal Wolsey had 230 beds there, mostly hung with silk and embroidery. At the end of the sixteenth century Holinshed states "Noblemen's houses have abundance of arras and rich tapestry hangings, otherwise the houses of knights and gentlemen have great provision of turkey work and tapestry. Many farmers have learned to garnish their cupboards with plate, their beds with tapestry and silk hangings, and their tables with carpets." In some houses an embroiderer would be employed as a resident member of the household staff, to repair, make new embroideries, and to weave. A large room would be set apart where women of the household could spend their leisure hours and take exercise during the winter months. Often this was in the form of a gallery running the entire length of the house. It was here that the embroidery would be done, usually on a square frame – the style of which has not changed in any way since that date. Mary Queen of Scots is known to have studied needlework in France and to have regularly employed her own designers, two of whom were Pierre Oudry and Charles Houvart. At this time there were few embroidery pattern books other than Italian ones, some of which were printed in England. A Booke of Curious and Strange Inventions, called the "First Part of Needleworkes" and pub-

lished in 1596, states that it was "imprinted in Venice, now newly printed for the gentlewomen of England." A quotation states "They must be careful, diligent and wise, in needleworkes that bear away the prise."

Other sources of design would be such books as "Gerard's Herbal," a catalogue of every known plant, with drawings and notes on its characteristics. The description of Mountain Mint reads, "It is applied to those that have the Sciatica or ache in the Huckle bone, for it draws the humor from the very bottom, and bringeth forth a comfortable heat to the whole joynt!" The first entirely English book for embroidery was "A Schole House for the Needle" by Richard Schorleyker, 1624. It illustrated the most usual motifs of the time, and included some lace and cut work. He began, "Here followeth certaine patterns of cut-workes, also sundry sorts of Spots, as Flowers, Birds, and Fishes, etc. and will fitly serve to be

14

16th century designs by Jacques le Moyne.

Designs from the
Thomas Trevellyan
manuscript in the
Folger Shakespeare
Library. These designs
had great influence on
the embroideries of
the period and may be
seen in many varia-
tions in Elizabethan
work.

Introduction

wrought, some with gould, some with silke, and some with crewell, or otherwise at your pleasure." These patterns were often transferred to the material by perforating the paper of the book directly, instead of first tracing the design. This may have led to the destruction of many books, and only two copies of Schorleyker are in existence today, both of them imperfect. In 1640 John Taylor, the water poet, wrote a book of poems to augment J. Boler's publication "The Needle's Excellency." (See p. 7.) The constant repetition of patterns with few variations in these books rather suggests that there were merchants supplying patterns already traced on the material. At this date the chief education of a girl consisted of reading, writing, music, singing, needlework and house-wifery. If more were needed, then skill in languages was acquired – and possibly drawing to beautify her needlework.

Because of the shortage of pattern books and the difficulty in obtaining designs by the average individual, the idea of the sampler originated. This meant that a record could be kept of a pattern and stitch, which could be remembered or shown to others. In early inventories records can be found of samplers and money purchases of material to make them. In a will proved at Boston in Lincolnshire in 1546 it is stated "I give to Alys Pynchebeck my sampler with semes". Often a narrow width of material was used, joined with decorative stitchery. Early undated samplers often had patterns arranged with no definite order on the fabric, and were collected as the occasion arose. In later ones the motifs were placed in orderly rows across the material.

Crewel Work was most usually done for bed-spreads, valances and curtains for four-poster beds, wall hangings, pockets, (two of which would be tied round the waist, under a dress), and petticoats. Examples of all these have been found nowadays, so obviously they were the most popular articles for wool embroidery, though other items, such as chair seats or curtains, may well have been worked in crewels but have long since worn out owing to their practical nature.

In England, "Jacobean" embroidery included not one but three main pattern arrangements.

17th century bed curtain showing Tree of Life design rising from hills with hounds, deer and butterflies.

Detail of a hanging with repeat design adapted from Elizabethan scroll designs.

Introduction

1. The Tree of Life design, taken directly from the East Indian palampores, and interpreted in many ways. These designs became so much in demand that large hangings were later embroidered (in exquisitely fine chain stitch) in India for commercial use.

2. The Elizabethan Scroll design. This consisted of an over-all pattern of sweeping stems, worked on a large scale, which curved around and almost enclosed the different flowers or leaves within them. The variation in motifs was unified by the strong dominating stem lines. (The typical Elizabethan Scroll design was usually finely worked in colored silks, or black and gold. During the reign of James I, however, the style developed into a bolder enlarged version and was worked in wool.)

3. A Wavy Border. This pattern arrangement came slightly later, and consisted of a wavy border enclosed with straight lines. This framed an area containing small motifs regularly sprigged within it.

In these later designs fewer stitches were used and the style was set by the brilliant colors and lighter, more open patterns. After 1750 silk was sometimes combined with the wool, or wool embroideries would have silk-quilted backgrounds. The light trend in design during Queen Anne's reign was carried on by Robert Adam, who designed embroidery for his own furniture, but by this time wool embroidery in England was superseded almost entirely by silk.

In America, however, the crewel fashion lasted longer, and it is hard to say where the English influence finished and American originality in design began. Certainly in the beginning designs were taken from pattern books like the English. Although there is practically nothing surviving which was worked before 1700 much must have been done before this date, as is evidenced by a Salem, Massachusetts, inventory of 1647 "A parcel of cruell thread and silk", and by another in 1654 mentioning "Cruell and fringe."

Although at first American designs were directly influenced by English ones, certain characteristics make the American easy to distinguish. The animals, flowers, and trees found in English and East

English 18th century bed curtain showing a wavy border design.

American 18th century bed curtain from Ipswich, Massachusetts, showing similar design with considerably lighter treatment.

Detail of a border for a petticoat, American 18th century. Chair seat cover, American 18th century, worked on linen and cotton twill with the nap still visible.

Indian designs were often transformed entirely, for the American embroideress stitched her petticoats and bed hangings with sheep, chickens, wild grapes and pine trees and all the things that were so much an integral part of her life.

This leads to the second difference, which is that American designs have a lightness and gaiety all their own. Perhaps part of their charm is that although the designs are balanced, they seldom have repeat motifs. The eye is led along flowing lines to discover one new detail after another, yet the whole has an over-all effect of unity. This exemplifies one of the great advantages embroidery has over a printed textile, namely – variety of stitch, color and texture, without repetition. It is therefore as exciting and interesting to work as it is delightful to look at. A con-

18th century petticoat, from Vermont, folded to show the design on the lower border.

18th century New England petticoat border.

Further detail of the petticoat. Notice how the shapes were traced and repeated –
the same squirrel appears in three different places and the cherry tree above is very
similar to the one on the chair seat of the preceding page. The embroiderer has simply
arranged set motifs to make her own delightful pastoral scene.

siderable number of the English examples must have been done in workrooms — their perfect technique and balanced proportions rather indicate a professional hand. The American ones were more apt to be worked by a farmer's wife most anxious to see her bed hangings completed, who would not be interested in embroidering endless repeat motifs. This may be what gives early American crewel its unique vitality and native charm. Moreover, American crewel was done to fill a definite need — as decorative fabrics were hard to come by, thus giving the designs an inherent strength and freshness that might have been lacking had the work been done for recreation alone.

An excellent example is a set of bed hangings worked by Mary Bulman, which is now at the Old Gaol Museum in York. Maine. Mary Bulman's husband travelled as a physician to William Pepperell, who was commander of the New England forces conducting the siege of Louisburg, Cape Breton Island, in 1745. It was there that Dr. Bulman died, leaving Mary a widow while still in her thirties. It is said that she may have started the embroidery to occupy her mind. All round the valance are embroidered verses, beautifully worked in trailing stitch, (a type of oversewing with padding underneath). One of them reads:

"Some of the fairest choirs above
Shall flock around my song
With Joy to hear the name they love
Sound from a mortal tongue."

The lovely design of flowers is carried out in fine worsteds with exquisite blending of the colors — pale pink shading to golden yellow, rose to deep crimson, for instance. The embroidery is done mainly in Roumanian stitch with the second step of the stitch being taken so long that it is almost the length of the first. This gives it the effect of a herringbone stitch worked very closely, and means that practically no material was taken up on the back of the work. This is yet another way of differentiating between English and American Crewel Work, for the early

Detail of the bed curtain from Ipswich, shown on page 19. This shows the closely worked effect of the right side, the stitching being carried out in Roumanian Stitch in fine crewels.

The wrong side of the work, showing how economical with wool the Roumanian Stitch could be. In New England this effect was sometimes called "two short stitches" because each band of stitches produces a narrow double row on the wrong side, as shown here.

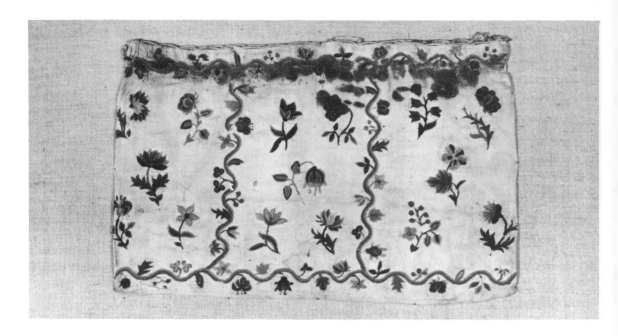

Work bag, 1747.

18th century pockets. Victoria and Albert Museum.

The 18th century Mary Bulman bed, in the Old Gaol Museum, York, Maine, is believed to be the only example in America complete with its hangings, valance and spread.

Detail of the embroidery

settlers had to be extremely economical with their wool. Therefore most of the stitches had to be done covering the largest possible area on the front of the linen and not wasting it on the back. Roumanian stitch was perfect for this purpose, so it was very widely used, and it is practically never found in English Crewel Work. The following is a list of stitches used by Mary Bulman on her bed hangings: Buttonhole – in close circles and as an outer edge softener, Roumanian, Herringbone – (open), Trailing, Crowsfeet – (three radiating stitches used as a powdering or open filling), Block Shading, Seeding, French Knots. It was customary for groups of ladies to meet in the afternoons to compare designs. At first a single color scheme was used. Every cottage had its tub of indigo at the back door into which the wool would be dipped for a certain length of time to produce deep blue, or less for the lighter shades. To begin with, threads, linens, and designs were imported, but later settlers spun, wove, and dyed many materials themselves. After indigo and white, a dull deep yellow or buff was the first home-dyed color to be introduced, but later came a complete range of colors, even mulberry and mauve from the iris, shades which were impossible to obtain before. The clarity, brilliance, and variety of these dyes are unequalled, even by the English Jacobean ones.

Just as they did in England, the ladies made themselves petticoats, pockets, chair seats, pocket books, and bed hangings. Because they were intended for practical use (even in the case of bed hangings, being cut down and later re-used as curtains or chair seats), all too few of these charming embroideries have been left to us today.

During the nineteenth century Crewel Work fell victim to the Industrial Revolution. The advent of roller printing and cheap woven fabrics ended the need for decoration by embroidery – and Crewel Work became a lost art.

Happily today, Crewel Embroidery is experiencing a great revival, partly due to the interest in restoration, but especially to the American woman's desire to work with her hands. She has rediscovered the joy of creating embroidery that is individual and imaginative, and like her forebears will produce heirlooms for future generations.

To Begin

You want to learn to do Crewel Embroidery. Perhaps you have a definite idea of what you want to make. You have an eighteenth century love seat which you have been wanting to cover for years. Or a set of dining room chairs which would be charming in a crewel work design that echoes the chintz of the dining room curtains. Or you have seen and admired a friend's cashmere sweater which you were certain came from Paris, only to be told she had embroidered it herself. Or perhaps you have simple modern furniture and want a set of throw pillows in brilliant colors and heavy wools. Last but not least, perhaps you just want to learn embroidery for fun, and look forward to spending absorbing hours with a new hobby. Whichever way it is – the best way is to start by making a sampler.

A bedspread could be worked in squares and joined together afterward. Opposite: a French chair calls for a light design; a flowering tree design would be suitable for an English wing chair.

Start by Making a Sampler

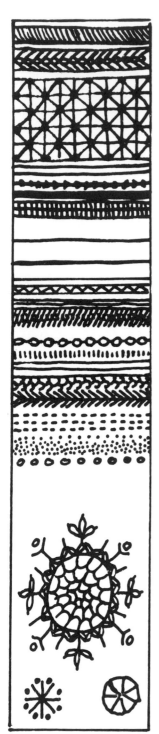

The word sampler came originally from the Latin word "Exemplar," to show, and that is exactly what it is. In this book you will find instructions for doing 64 stitches. Each one of these stitches may be varied in many ways by working with heavy or fine thread, by embroidering the stitches open or closely together and of course by changing color. So it is a good idea to have samples of some of these variations all on one strip of fabric. Then you may refer to it from time to time, just like a recipe book, when you are working on a specific project and trying to decide which stitch to put where.

To make a sampler, all you need are a few crewel wools, some embroidery needles, possibly a ring frame,* and last but not least, the material. A half a yard of linen is fine. This is best to practice on if it is closely woven, so you can't do better than buy linen twill, or a piece of ordinary pillow ticking. Because of the diagonal weave both are very firm materials and your stitches will be neat and clear. In the case of the ticking you can use the stripes as part of the design too.

The child's jacket shown opposite page 32 in color and on page 33 in black and white was worked as a sampler. The stripes may be followed instead of having to draw a design, and the ticking showing through the embroidery in places gives an interesting effect. The sampler might also be made up afterwards into an envelope handbag, a draw-string workbag, a belt or even a pair of slippers.

The stitches shown on the front of the jacket (in color) are the following, reading from left to right:

1. Buttonhole (2 rows back to back, interlaced afterward)
2. Chain
3. Raised Chain
4. Couching
5. Stem (several rows close together)
6. Interlaced Running Stitch
7. Coral
8. Threaded Back Stitch
9. Close Herringbone
10. Pekinese
11. Zig-zag Chain

* See Page 49 Wools and Needles; also see Page 50 Color. Page 42 Frames

Start by Making a Sampler

12. Rosette Chain
13. Fishbone Stitch (leaves with flowers of 3 Detached Chain Stitches and 3 French Knots)
14. Detached Twisted Chain (interlaced)
15. Van Dyke
16. Crossed Satin Stitch
17. Close Herringbone

The stitches then repeat out from the center front in reverse order.

The stitches used on the back of the jacket (page 33) are:

Braid
Buttonhole
Cretan (open)
Roumanian
Chain (worked as a wavy line)
Fishbone (open)
Herringbone
French Knots
Ziz-zag Chain

Satin (slanting)
Rope
Roumanian
Split Stitch (worked in close rows)
Interlaced Herringbone
Cable Chain
Seeding Straight Stitch
Spider's Webs (woven)
Buttonhole (2 rows back to back)

Using simple materials such as linen twill or ticking is really the best way at first.

There is plenty of time later to get involved with heavy slub linens, wool tweeds, or antique satins, when you set about making a definite item. Then you will need to choose carefully from the many varieties on the market today, both for suitability (so that your fabric is either a background or an integral part of the design which does not try to dominate), and for wearing qualities. Here are a few suggestions — you will be able to add to the list after experimenting yourself.

The drawings on these pages show different ways of arranging a narrow sampler to which you may add as you go along.

Choosing Fabrics

FOR CHAIR SEATS, FOOTSTOOLS, WING ARMCHAIRS, ETC.

Use linen twill, closely woven worsted or wool tweed, or any material which is closely woven and not too variegated in texture to interfere with the embroidery. Material should be very strong for anything which is to receive wear and which is tightly stretched over a foundation, so be careful of some weaves which include synthetics – as some of these might not have the same durability as natural fibers.

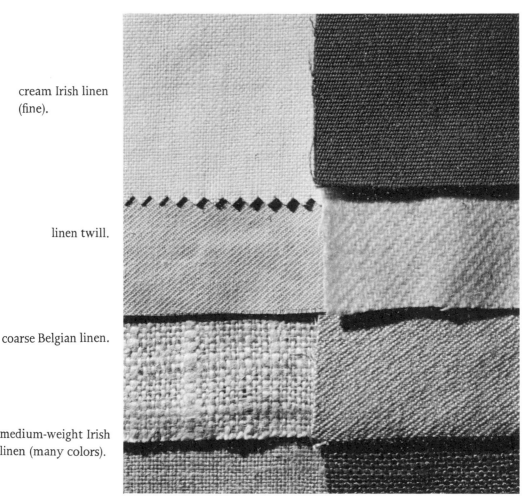

cream Irish linen (fine).

all wool worsted (many colors).

linen twill.

twill-weave wool.

coarse Belgian linen.

antique satin.

medium-weight Irish linen (many colors).

stub linen (many colors).

Child's vest, worked as a sampler on pillow ticking

Four cushions
illustrating
a variety
of designs

Child's jacket worked on ticking; the stitches used are listed on page 31.

FOR CURTAINS, BED-SPREADS, ETC.
(where the material will hang loosely)

Use Irish linen, homespun or hand-woven linen (if obtainable), antique satin or linen twill. Cotton or silk fabrics (unless mixed with other fibers) are generally too closely woven for the thickness of the wool — the needle will not draw through easily and the material will pucker.

FOR WALL HANGINGS, MIRROR FRAMES, PICTURES

Use any of the above materials, plus burlap, or any of the new "mixtures." Here the choice is much freer as the article will not receive hard wear.

Having obtained a simple ½ yd. of fabric for your sampler, however, the next stage is to begin the design.

Beginning the Design

Even though this is a sampler, it is best to work it in a design of some form, so that you can practice fitting the stitches into different shapes. Every moment is valuable, so it seems a pity to waste time on an embroidery which will lie in a drawer afterwards. Aim at making it into something you could use – a pillow, a telephone book cover – or plan it like one of the long strip samplers of the eighteenth century – adding things as you go along. Then you may even want to hang it on the wall afterwards!

Sketch out your pattern on "Layout" paper. The latter is better than tracing paper because it is heavier and yet you can see well enough to trace through it. A pad of it is obtainable from most art stores in all sizes. The largest made will be the most practical.

Divide the material in the simplest way possible so that the stitches can be varied without making the whole design confused. One idea is to draw a few basic lines, in a random pattern, then work out the rest as you go along, being guided by the stitches themselves. Otherwise you can make a geometric design which will give you practice at finding similar stitches to balance one another at opposite sides. Still another idea is to work the sampler in two halves, with all the close solid stitches on one side and the open ones on the other. Pillow ticking is of course the simplest of all, for within the restrictions of narrow banding you can use any stitches you choose. Having settled the form your sampler is to take, the next stage will consist of applying the pattern.

A sampler used mainly to
show open fillings.
Starting at the top and
reading from left to right :
Squared Fillings #5, #4.
Circles of Weaving Stitch
and Satin Stitch with 8
Bullion Knots.
Squared Fillings #3, #6.
#2.
Squared Fillings #1, #10,
#9,
Squared Fillings #8, #7.
Whipped Spider's Web (in
two colors), Raised Weav-
ing Stitch with French
Knots, Woven Spider's Web
(in two colors).

Applying the Pattern

There are several good ways of doing this. The first and easiest way is by

USING DRESSMAKERS' CARBON

Buy a packet of dressmakers' carbon from any notion department or sewing supply shop. (Ordinary carbon will smudge.) Fold the material in half and then half again, and crease the folds so that they show clearly. If the material happens to be crease-resistant, baste the center lines in both directions with a contrasting color thread. Then smooth the material flat on a table or board and hold it down evenly with masking tape on all four sides (as shown). A really smooth hard surface is necessary.

Fold the design, too, into four equal parts, and lay it down, still folded, so that it fits into one quarter of the fabric (as shown). Without shifting the paper, carefully unfold the design. The folds marking the center of the material and the paper will now be as one, and you will know the design is placed exactly in the middle. (Of course you must be sure your design was in the center of the folded paper first!)

Now slide a sheet of carbon paper, face downwards, between paper and material. Use blue carbon for light materials, white for dark ones. Anchor the paper with some heavy weights (books, paperweights, etc.) and trace round the outline *very heavily* with a pencil. Using weights is a better idea than taping the design all round, because you can lift a corner occasionally to see how well the carbon is transferring. You really must *engrave* heavily to get good results, but you will soon find this out as you work.

The two drawbacks to this method are: (1) The design is often spoiled by the heavy pencil marks, and (2) Some materials will not take the carbon easily. Therefore, especially when the design is to be used more than once, there is no more accurate method of transferring a design than by making a pricking.

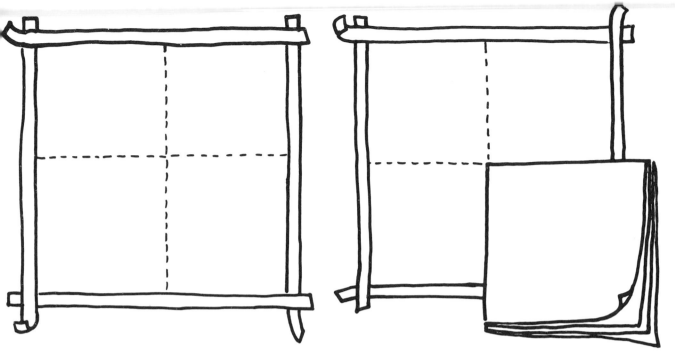

Having folded the material, lay it out and fasten down with masking tape.

Fold the design into four parts and place it in position on one quarter of the fabric.

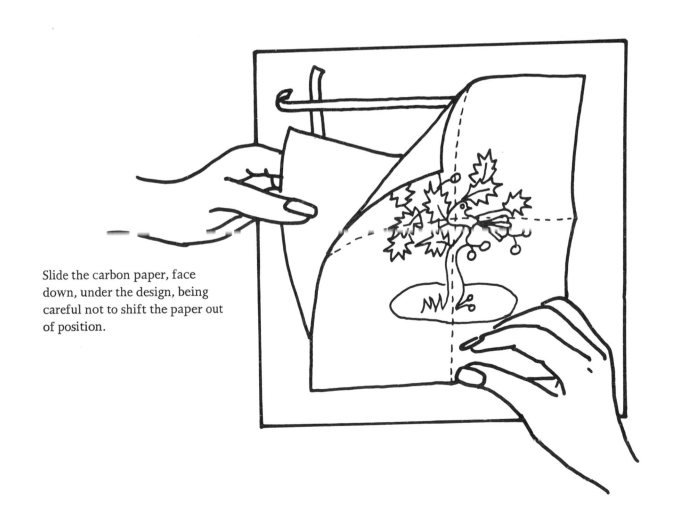

Slide the carbon paper, face down, under the design, being careful not to shift the paper out of position.

Applying the Pattern

MAKING A PRICKING

(1) Break a needle in half and set it into the eraser of an ordinary pencil. You will have to push the needle, blunt end first, into the eraser with a pair of pliers, then you will have a nice short pointed spike sticking out.

(2) Trace the design onto a piece of layout or stout tracing paper, lay this over a pad of felt, or any thick layer of material, placing a sheet of tissue between the two. Now prick holes with your spiked pencil, all around the outlines, holding the pencil vertically – the holes should be fine and close, but as you practice your hand becomes like a machine, working fast and evenly.

(3) First fold both fabric and pricking in four to find the center and hold it in place with weights (as in the carbon method). At a drugstore buy some *powdered* charcoal, and with a rolled and stitched pad of felt, or a blackboard eraser, rub the charcoal through the pricking you have made. Do this quite lightly, rubbing in a circular direction, without using too much charcoal. Lift a corner of the design to check, and if the line is not clear, rub through a little more "pounce" as the charcoal is called. If there is too much already, lift off the pricking and lightly blow off the surplus, leaving a clear line to follow with a brush.

(4) Using a fine watercolor brush (#3 or #4) and a tube of blue watercolor paint, or gouache, paint around all the outlines. You will find the right mixture with practice—too much water, and the line will run, too much paint and it will not flow at all! Always begin at the edge nearest you, covering what you have done with a sheet of tissue paper, so that the pounce will not be smudged by your hand rubbing it. If you do not feel very much like an artist use a ballpoint pen instead. Draw a line with the pen on the corner of the material and test the ink in water first to see if it is fast. On dark material use white watercolor or gouache instead. Finally, bang the design hard with a clean cloth to remove the surplus charcoal – rubbing will smudge it, so flick it until it is clean.

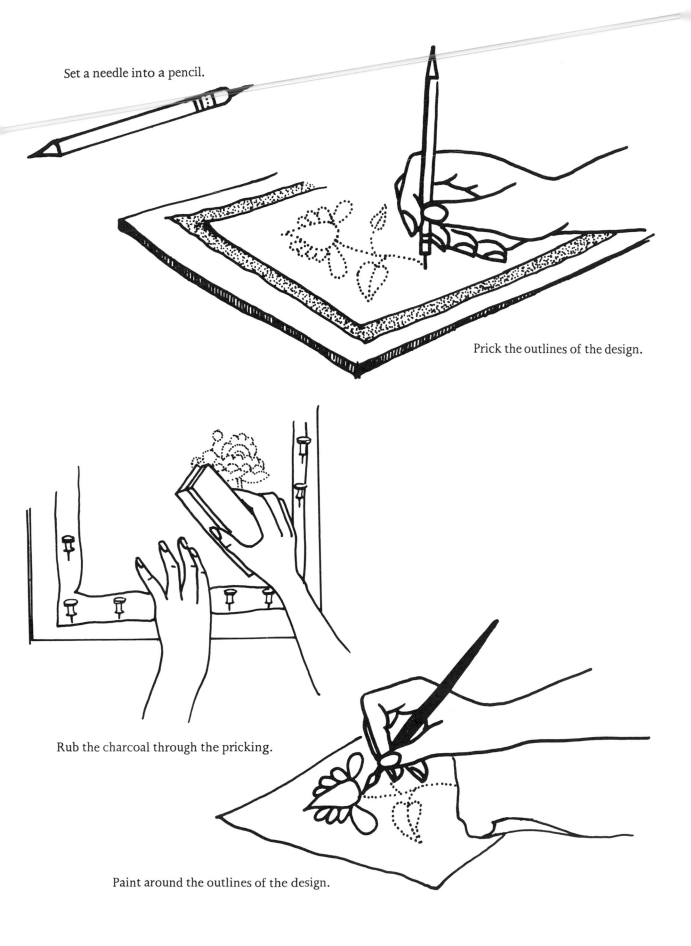

Set a needle into a pencil.

Prick the outlines of the design.

Rub the charcoal through the pricking.

Paint around the outlines of the design.

Applying the Pattern

APPLYING THE DESIGN WITH A TRANSFER PENCIL

This product has arrived on the market lately and is a good short-cut. Using the pink transferring pencil, outline the design on layout or tracing paper, then turn it face downwards onto the material and iron like an ordinary commercial transfer, using a fairly warm iron. The one disadvantage is that it is apt to rub off and it does not provide a very clear fine line. It is therefore most useful for larger bold designs.

Certain fluffy materials, such as wool sweaters, for instance, will not take either paint or carbon well. In this case the only satisfactory method is:

APPLYING THE DESIGN WITH BASTING STITCHES

Buy some batiste, organdie or chiffon, and trace the design through the transparent material, using a hard pencil (of course method 1 and 2 may also be used for this equally well if desired.)

Pin the material with the design to the inside of the sweater. Then baste all around the outlines with small running stitches, using a contrasting color thread. The design will then be transferred onto the right side, and may be embroidered right over the running stitches to cover them.

Applying the Pattern

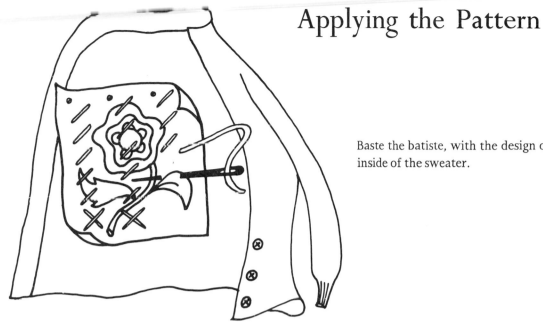

Baste the batiste, with the design on it, to the inside of the sweater.

Baste around the outlines of the design, taking larger stitches on the wool side than on the batiste side.

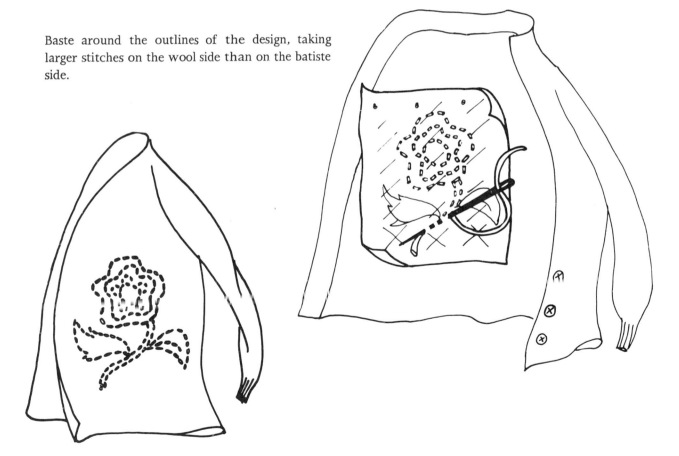

Finished design, showing on the right side in basting stitches, ready to start work. Surplus batiste may be trimmed away on the wrong side after the design has been embroidered.

Choosing a Frame

First of all, is a frame really necessary? If you want to have fun doing a variety of stitches, and your work is to be neat and even, then some sort of frame is a necessity. In fact, it is almost as indispensable as a loom is to a weaver. There are several types to choose from, however. The most useful is probably the ring frame with a floor stand, illustrated here. The ring can be fitted over any section of the work, because the Crewel Work and the linen are tough enough not to be harmed by it, so that a piece of embroidery of any size can be worked. The stand allows you to sit comfortably, working with both hands, one above and one below the frame, necessary for speed and rhythm. When you begin stitching you will find that using your left hand (or right if you are left-handed) feels extraordinary at first, but if you stick to it in the beginning you will be quite used to it after only about an hour of working. After a few days you'll be doing it automatically, and after a week you won't be able to use one hand only!

The other similar variety of frame, equally good, is a ring frame with a table clamp. As shown, it screws on to a table or the arm of a chair, is adjustable as to height and has the advantage of being small enough to carry about. The only disadvantage sometimes is finding a convenient table and not being able to leave the work set up. The floor variety stands in the corner of the room inviting you to sew during the odd ten minutes during the day which are so often wasted. Ring frames *are* made without stands or clamps, and are certainly better than nothing

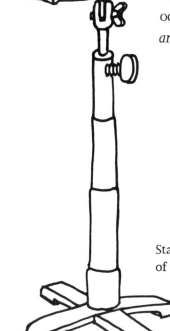

Standing floor frame, adjustable to height and angle of working.

at all, but they should have an adjustable screw so that the material can be pulled as tight as a drum (essential for all frames) and should be made of wood rather than metal as the latter does not grip well.

The third kind of ring frame is the one which has its own stand, and will rest on a table, or your lap. The advantages of this one are obvious – it is so easy to move about, and is small and compact as well. But the disadvantage of it is that it is inclined to wobble, especially if it is standing on a table – though a heavy book placed on the stand helps to correct this.

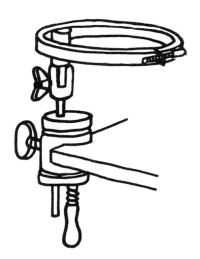

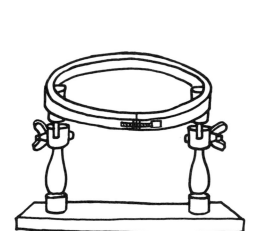

Lap frame, which will stand on a table, with adjustable angle of working.

Table tambour frame, adjustable to height and angle of working.

Simple hoop frame, made of wood, not metal, with a screw adjustment which is best for holding the material really taut.

Choosing a Frame

MOUNTING THE MATERIAL INTO A RING FRAME

First remove the outer hoop of the frame. Lay the material over the inner ring with that part of the design which is to be worked exposed in the center. Tighten the screw of the outer hoop so that it fits down over both the inner ring and the material very snugly. Do not press the hoop all the way down, just push it on so that it fits firmly all round, (as shown in the diagram). The next step is to pull the fabric taut, while simultaneously pressing down on the rim of the frame with your palms, (as shown). Work right round the perimeter in this way until the material is stretched like a drum. Finally press down the outer hoop. It need not be absolutely flat as long as the material is taut.

Wool embroidery on linen is firm enough not to be crushed by having the frame pushed over it when the design has to be moved. The

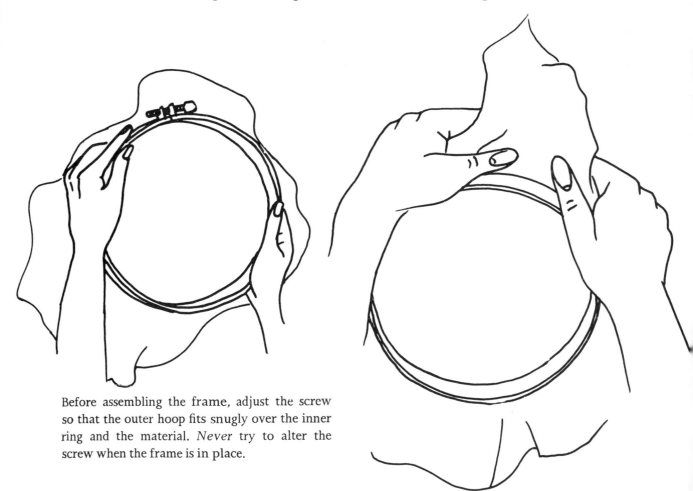

Before assembling the frame, adjust the screw so that the outer hoop fits snugly over the inner ring and the material. *Never* try to alter the screw when the frame is in place.

Pull the material taut; if the upper ring is tight enough the material will not slip back.

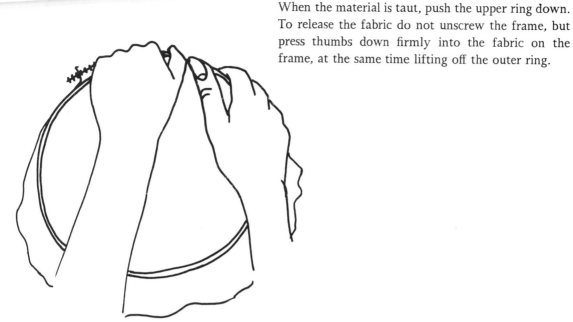

When the material is taut, push the upper ring down. To release the fabric do not unscrew the frame, but press thumbs down firmly into the fabric on the frame, at the same time lifting off the outer ring.

only stitches which might be disturbed are Bullion Knots . . . so it is best to work them last if possible. Delicate fabrics, or those with a satin weave, *may* be marked by the hoop, so place layers of tissue paper over the design before pushing the frame down. Then tear the paper away from the surface of the work, leaving it protecting the fabric round the edge where the hoop would be liable to chafe it.

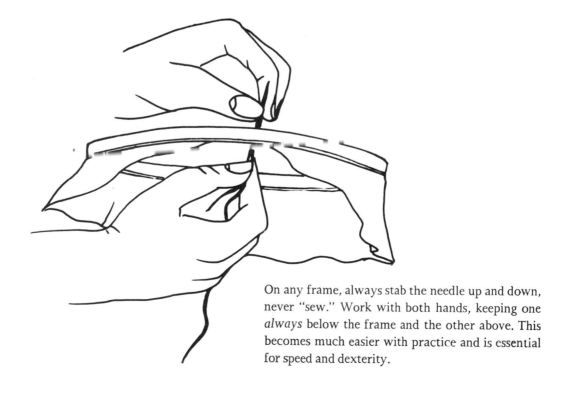

On any frame, always stab the needle up and down, never "sew." Work with both hands, keeping one *always* below the frame and the other above. This becomes much easier with practice and is essential for speed and dexterity.

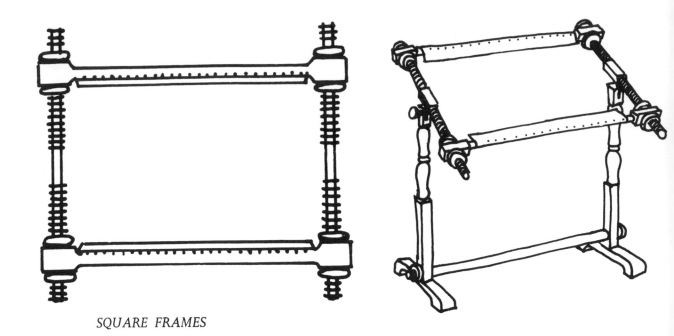

SQUARE FRAMES

Then there are square frames (illustrated). These are delightful to work on since the material is always beautifully taut. They *must* be used for certain materials: damask, upholstery satin, etc., might be marked or rubbed by the ring of the tambour frames, for instance. The disadvantage of a square frame is that it is awkward to move about. Secondly, it will only take material of the same width as itself. The length may be rolled round the rollers, but the width can only be that of the frame, 18″, 24″ or 36″ (average frame sizes.) So that it is impossible to work a large bed-spread on a square frame without having the frame made up to a special size.

It is perfectly possible, of course, to do crewel embroidery in your hand. The only disadvantage is that certain stitches are eliminated from your repertoire. You cannot lay long threads across a surface, and tie them down afterwards, for instance, unless you have a firm foundation to work on. A great many people do extremely neat work without using a frame at all, but for the average person, a good effect is far more easily gained with its help. When using either a table or floor ring frame and both hands, the speed, dexterity, and ease with which you work will surprise you. The stitches for which a frame is essential are marked with an asterisk throughout this book – all others can be worked with or without it.

Choosing a Frame

MOUNTING WORK IN A SQUARE FRAME

(1) Begin by marking the center of the webbing with pencil, on both sides of the frame. Crease a ¼" turning on the two opposite edges of the material to be mounted in the frame, then crease these edges in the center – or measure them and then mark the middle with a pin. Working with the frame towards you, place the creased center of the material to the marked webbing, and pin the two together vertically. Then, beginning in the middle, with strong linen thread in the needle, whip the material and the webbing together with shallow stitches. Do not take the stitches too deep, or a ridge will be formed which will mark the material when the frame is rolled. Starting in the center and working out to either edge insures that the material will still be centered by the time the whipping is finished. Sew both opposite sides in this way. End off firmly by taking several stitches back over the previous ones to form crosses.

(2) Now assemble the frame by twisting both inner screws on the side arms, to the middle. Slip the main part of the frame, with the material rolled uppermost, onto the side arms, and turn the screws out again until the frame is taut. Be sure both sides are stretched equally – measure or count the threads of the side arms. Place the outer screws in position to hold the frame firm.

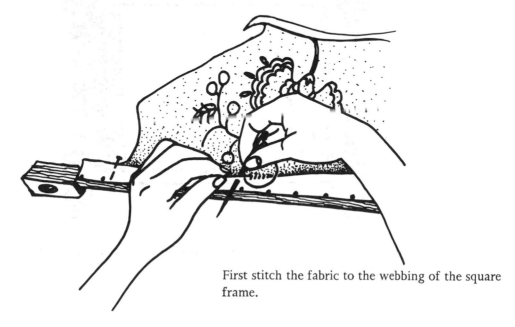

First stitch the fabric to the webbing of the square frame.

Choosing a Frame

Now sew a strip of webbing or heavy tape to either side of the material. Using double linen thread, start with a knot and take a series of horizontal stitches, moving the needle down about an inch between each. This produces a slanting diagonal stitch on the front and is very firm. Begin and end off with one or two cross stitches. Finally with an upholstery or packing needle (large and curved) and some stout string, lace the sides, going *down* through the webbing, up around the arm of the frame and down through the webbing again. Work from left to right. Secure the left-hand end by twisting the string around the arms several times (as shown) and knotting it to itself with a half bow (which can be easily undone when adjusting the frame.) Pull up on the string equally on both sides until the frame is really firm and even, and fasten the string as before. The fabric must be stretched like a drum, for nothing is worse than a spongy frame to work on – it is almost better to have none at all. During working it may loosen, so a twist or two of the screws, or a pull on the string, will tighten it again. The frame may be rested against a table when working, but it is also available with its own trestles to support it.

Stitch the webbing to the sides of the frame. Here the right-hand side has already been laced with string.

Wools and Needles

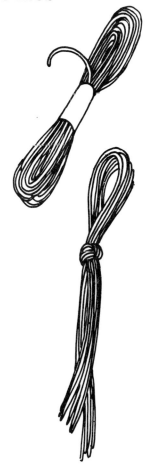

Real crewel wool is two-ply wool, firm and not too "stretchy," put out in small hanks with a good variety of colors. There are no rules about whether you should use one, two or more threads for certain stitches. You can vary the number entirely according to the effect you want, light or heavy. This is the advantage of having a fine wool to begin with. Experience and practice will help you decide, and you will find that varying the thickness often in one piece of work helps to create an interesting change of texture, as does combining silk (mercerized cotton will do equally well) with the wool in parts of the design. The beginner always tends to work too tightly. This stretches the wool too much and makes it thin. Experience produces a more even tension, and this difficulty will be overcome – but it can also be avoided at the beginning if short lengths of thread are used, and a needle that is large enough for the thickness of the wool.

Needles should be of medium length but with long eyes. These are available at most stores and come in packets of assorted sizes called either "Crewel" or "Embroidery." Don't make a mistake and buy darners, because though they have large eyes, they are far too long and difficult to handle. When stabbing in and out on a frame your fingers do not hold a long needle near enough to the point and therefore cannot control it properly. Tapestry (blunt) needles are needed too for stitches which are worked mostly on the surface of the material and only occasionally pass through it, such as Weaving Stitch, Spider's Webs, Pekinese, etc. The higher the number the finer the needle. For instance, the finest crewel needle you would need for wool work would be #8, a good average size is #5, and for very heavy work #3 or #4. In a tapestry needle use #21 or buy a packet of assorted sizes. The needle should always be slightly thicker than the thread, to open up a passage for it to pass through easily – without this, constant passing back and forth will wear out the wool and it will break.

3 – 8

Color

The hardest thing when you are confronted with a glorious array of colors, is to choose and eliminate. The first and most common error in thinking is, "leaves *must* be green, carnations must be pink or white, whoever heard of a purple fish?" etc.! The answer is, of course, if your design is stylized enough, any motif can be any color. Think of a willow pattern plate – blue trees, bridges, houses, people. This is perfect for embroidery, because the simpler the color scheme the more varied can the stitches be without the result becoming too "busy." The easiest way to start is to experiment with several shades of one color (dark, medium or light). Another easy and very effective way is to use all the varieties of one type of color, red, pink, rust, orange, or blue-green, royal blue, blue, purple etc. If you are going to use many colors, pick out the basic ones and let one color predominate, or choose one brilliant color for accent to be used sparingly. Don't be afraid of colors. They never look as bright when they are worked as when they are in the skein. Practice and experience are the only guides here, and the more embroidery you do, the more you will become conscious of color all around you – things like flower arrangements, chintzes, or a turkey carpet will all give you inspiration. Look at your favorite print dress – it is apt to be a color arrangement designed by a professional. If you think that blue and green are not compatible with one another, look at nature and notice how wonderful a green tree looks against the blue sky. The same goes for pinks, reds and oranges as in a sunset. There are no hard and fast rules, yet embroidery with wools is easier than painting – the colors are already there – they don't have to be mixed. It's a good plan to lay out the skeins of wool all over the design before you start, and if necessary move them about – add colors, or take away. This is safer than making a painting to follow – so often the wools cannot be matched to the exact colors in the painting, and the whole effect is lost. A sketch with the dark, medium or light areas roughly put in with either paints or crayon is a great help. This will teach you to look for tone values in colors and then you will know where you want to put the darker more intense colors and vice versa.

Wing armchair worked in wool on linen twill, showing contemporary treatment of a typical early English design

The embroidery on this 18th century armchair is a modern adaptation of a French scrolling stem design worked in fine wools

Color

Stitches make a great difference here too. The same color used for a closely worked stitch can look twice as dark or bright as the identical color used for an open one.

An 18th century American bed-spread worked entirely in shades of blue. With this simple color scheme contrasts are obtained by working a balance of light powdering stitches and close solid ones.

The Stitches

Today the world is growing smaller — countries interchange goods of all kinds and in America so many things are brought from every corner of the globe that sometimes their origins are quite forgotten. In the same way, crewel stitches today borrow from the heritage of every country's tradition. Stem-stitch — the twisted stitch combined with the weaving of Coptic and New Zealand garments — perhaps the first 'stitch' ever embroidered, herringbone stitch from the Greek Islands, the Roumanian group of 'banding' stitches, such as Mosoul, **Van Dyke** and fishbone — used to completely cover the material in the Baltic and Mediterranean peasant costumes; split stitch and couching from England (from the famous 'Opus Anglicanum' church vestments which were exported all over Europe in the 12th century). Laid work from Italy, chain stitch from India, what a marvellous freedom and wealth of ideas is ours today. Traditional Jacobean embroidery used many of these stitches, notably long and short, chain, satin, stem, French knots, coral, herringbone, squared fillings, seeding, bullion knots, laid work, couching, back stitch, wave stitch, block shading, braid stitch, fly stitch, detached chain and cross stitch — to list those on a few well-known embroideries. This does not mean that others were not used, but the most usual were the first nine.

Early American work developed its own style although it used several stitches in common with the English. In a great many cases instead of long and short stitch, Roumanian stitch was used. Sometimes a whole piece of work would be embroidered in this alone, worked in bands fitted closely together and covering the entire motif. French knots and seeding were sometimes used for small details. On the whole the stitches were fewer and simpler than the English pieces — possibly because much of it must have been done without a frame.

However, just as we do not, today, want to make an exact copy of an 'Opus Anglicanum' cope, so we need not be slaves of tradition, following the ideas of another century. The great thing is to learn all the stitches, so that we have a fund of them at our command, then choose and eliminate, experiment, select, and discard until we have found the perfect stitches to express each design best.

This chair was worked in rust, grey greens, ochre and stone colors, to balance a chintz in the same room. The stitches are simple, mainly Chain, Stem, Buttonhole and Roumanian, with Spider's Webs, French and Bullion Knots for small details.

The Stitches

54

Which comes first?

The hen or the egg?

The design or the stitches?

Many advocates of a free contemporary style suggest starting with a stitch and letting it guide your fancy as you go along. This is a reaction to the mass-produced transfers and partially finished embroideries still unfortunately on sale in many department stores. The lack of imagination and bad taste are enough to quench the spirit of any would-be creative embroiderer. But I feel there is a mid-way course. Once you have done a certain amount of experiment on your sampler, and have become aware of the many sources of inspiration, ideas shouldn't be

This tree was worked with leaves of block shading and French Knot fruits; Burden Stitch to suggest bark on the trunk, and Raised Stem Stitch to give the effect of a wattle fence.

The free adaptation of an early American design for this screen lent itself to a great variety of stitches on a bold scale. The baskets were first worked on canvas and then appliquéed to the fabric.

This chair shows a design of scattered motifs filling a space, allowing more variety of stitch and color than an over-all flowing design. The colors used were greens, yellows, bright reds, pinks and pale blues.

hard to find. If you have had an idea and mapped it out on paper with the limitations of embroidery in mind as you draw, you can decide what sort of stitches you would like for the design. Don't be overwhelmed by the many waiting to be used. No matter which ones you choose when it comes down to the basic elements there are only three ways of using them. Closely for a solid bold effect, widely spaced for lacy open effect, or a happy combination of the two (the most difficult!). A few stitches look best worked open, a few can only be worked solidly, but most are very adaptable and will do either at your will. Simplification is the golden rule, don't try to be too detailed or lose sight of the over-all effect. You are representing an idea, not imitating it. Once you have found the key to translating a form into stitches you can apply it to any design – your eye will become trained to notice and select everything it needs.

The color scheme will influence your choice because when it is mono-chromatic full play can be given to the solid and open effects of the stitches – the same applies to a limited color scheme. This does not mean that a simple pattern might not be extremely effective worked entirely in one stitch and one color. But in these days of enormous variety in printed and woven textiles it is perhaps more interesting to work and look at as an embroidery if there is variation in one or the other. When many colors *and* many stitches are used, though, the result can be over-bearing and fussy unless the design has strong dominating lines or motifs of repeating stitch or color to hold everything together.

Take a plunge and make a start on things you *know* are safe, using the color and stitch you know you want to predominate. Leave the accents for last in small quantities – one brilliant spot of color, or a very few openwork stitches in a closely massed design, or a few wider dominant lines to give character to a uniformly open pattern – and so on. Whatever you do, you will have to experiment and change your ideas as you go along. Experience counts tremendously but even after a great deal of practice it is not always possible to decide which stitch is best the first time. However, don't unpick too much at first! It is much

The Stitches

better to complete a piece of work and look back later, decide what was wrong with it and improve on the next, than to try and have the first design absolutely perfect right away.

Some specific stitches useful for solidly filling a pattern (any one of the following stitches may be used individually for an entire design):

Chain Stitch	Block Shading
Roumanian Stitch	Long and Short
Stem Stitch	Laid Work
Split Stitch	

Some specific stitches useful for openwork fillings:

French Knots	Cloud Stitch
Bullion Knots	Squared Fillings
Herringbone Stitch	Burden Stitch
Wave Stitch	Seeding

A handbag, showing an equal balance of open and solid filling stitches. It is worked in blues, greens and pale yellows, using mainly Burden Stitch, Laid Work, Long and Short Stitch, Fishbone Stitch, Padded Satin Stitch and Seeding.

This tree makes a good sampler as the leaves
and fruits are worked with many variations
of solid filling stitches, sufficiently alike not to
detract from the balance of the whole design.

A contemporary adaptation of the Elizabethan scrolling pattern, using the fruits of
New York State instead of traditional flowers. Close solid stitches make it practical
for the hard wear of a stool seat.

Stretching and Blocking

When the sampler is finished it may be pressed or blocked. The latter is preferable, for pressing never brings out the very fine creases in heavy material like twill, and pressing is also inclined to pull the article out of shape. If, however, you wish to press an article such as a sweater which cannot be blocked, iron it on the wrong side into three or four thicknesses of towelling, using a damp cloth or steam iron. To block the finished work, first soak the embroidery in cold water, and lay it, dripping wet, on a board or old table which has been first covered with a sheet. If the embroidery is raised, lay it out right side uppermost, if it is flat and a smooth finished result is needed, lay it right side downwards. Then with carpet tacks, nail down the four corners first, measuring the opposite sides to see that they are even and making sure the corners are true right angles. You may have to pull the material out with pliers to make sure it is really taut. Then nail down four more tacks, one in the center of each side, and then eight more in the spaces between. Continue round and round, adding in this way more tacks until they are about a quarter of an inch apart. Allow the fabric to dry. When it is thoroughly dry, take it up, and if it is not being mounted immediately, roll it round a cardboard tube with the embroidery outwards (so that the stitches are not crushed against one another).

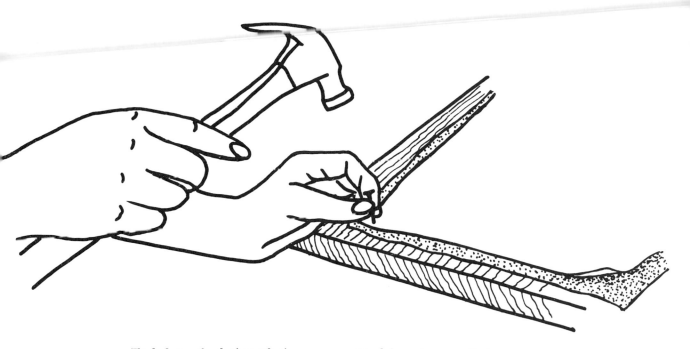

Tack down the design, placing one carpet tack in each corner first.

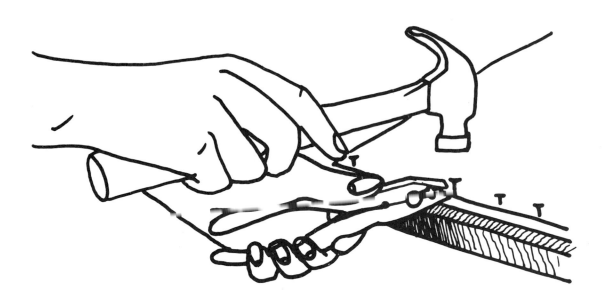

Tack the fabric all around, pulling it out flat with pliers so that it is really taut.

Designs for Individual Projects

DESIGNS WITH CUT-OUT SHAPES

Now you have a sampler finished. You have chosen the material, and you know exactly what you want to make. All you need is the *design*. This may seem a large blank area in your mind. Where to begin? First you need inspiration. The more embroidery you do, the more aware you will become of the possibilities for design, and constant practice at noticing things, and converting them in your mind's eye into an embroidery pattern will open a new world.

You can start slowly – no need to be frightened at having to launch out into the completely unknown to begin with. You have designed your sampler perhaps with very simple lines and geometric shapes. This should have taught you a lesson in space filling, which is that the spaces between the shapes are as important as the shapes themselves. In other words the background material showing through is part of the finished design, and the over-all effect of the *whole* is the important thing. It is a good idea to cut out shapes in paper and arrange them in juxtaposition to one another until you like the arrangement best. Shapes will show off the stitches well if they are simple and stylized, rather than naturalistic or photographic. You can cut out squares, triangles, circles, or indeed any simple forms in colored paper. Arrange them to overlap or fall into groups, and change them freely until the design pleases you. Or you can fold a square of paper in half four or five times. Cut shapes through all the folded thicknesses, and open up the paper again to form a kaleidoscopic pattern.

In all cases keep the design simple, so that the eye is held and led on to the next place easily without being confused by too many motifs competing with one another.

Also, remember the over-all effect, so that the space is filled without leaving large unintentional blank areas or being too overcrowded and cluttered. Study the space the design is to fill, whether it is a circle, an oblong, square, or irregular shape, and arrange the design accordingly

Cut-out designs from folded paper.

This appliquéed quilt shows how simple silhouettes might be filled with suitable repeat stitches most effectively. The stylized shapes mean that full play may be given to the stitches.

64

Martha Washington chair, showing Mt. Vernon and other appropriate motifs.

Designs for Individual Projects

Never forget that you are making an embroidery – something that is to look better in stitchery than any other medium. The main purpose of embroidery is to represent, not to imitate, so keep the design stylized

Vest with birds worked with very little shading, mainly in Chain, Split and Satin Stitches.

Designs for Individual Projects

and not photographic. This means observation and elimination; it will show off the stitches to their best advantage, and will also be much more fun to work. Unless the design is completely abstract, do not break the basic laws of nature. For instance, stems and branches never grow downwards from their main stem at an acute angle. Petals radiate from a central axis, and so on. In other words, if natural forms, however stylized, look as though they could grow, the design will have more strength.

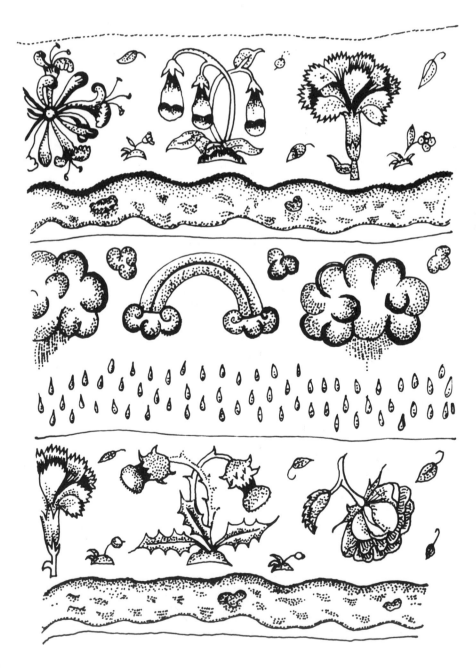

An Elizabethan sleeve worked in outline and seeding stitches, showing stylized rain clouds and rainbow.

A design suitable for a pillow uses a wide variety of solid stitches, including Long and Short Stitch, Block Shading, Shaded Laid Work and Burden Stitch.

Embroideries drawn from designs in Victoria and Albert Museum.

The simple outlines here allow different filling stitches to be used within them. Notice the double outlines separating the patterns clearly yet lightly.

One of a series of 17th century embroideries illustrating Biblical subjects. Notice the water carried out in Stem Stitch and how simple and effective it is.

Designs for Individual Projects

TASTE AND IDEAS

A great many books have been published lately concerning the subject of design for embroidery. The authors without exception cry with one voice, "Everyone can draw!" "Design your own work," they say. "Do not rely on hackneyed mass-produced transfers; it's not easy, but practice makes perfect." One author claims that if we had all had as much practice at designing as we have at writing, we could jot down a design as easily as writing "coffee" on our shopping list. This is not necessarily true! With superb optimism, they believe that after reading a few brief instructions one can become a brilliant creative designer. But the truth of the matter is that just as clothes are an expression of our individual taste, and only a few of us make *and* design them ourselves, so the same holds good for embroidery. While originality in design is

A pillow and the chintz from which the design was adapted. Notice how much more definite the shapes have to be to make a satisfactory embroidery.

One of a pair of pillows adapted from an 18th century wallpaper in Williamsburg. The colors are terra cotta, brown, dull green and gold.

A design with half an orange in the center, inspired by an 18th century teapot.

Designs for Individual Projects

delightful, there is no harm in drawing inspiration from beautiful historic examples, or from a work of art, and re-creating from them your own embroidery. The artistic expression lies in your free interpretation and your choice of color and stitch. The main idea is being able to differentiate between good and bad, and training the eye to be alert to all the sources of inspiration. Part of the fun of the whole thing is gradually learning what to look for and which design will best suit the limitations of embroidery stitches.

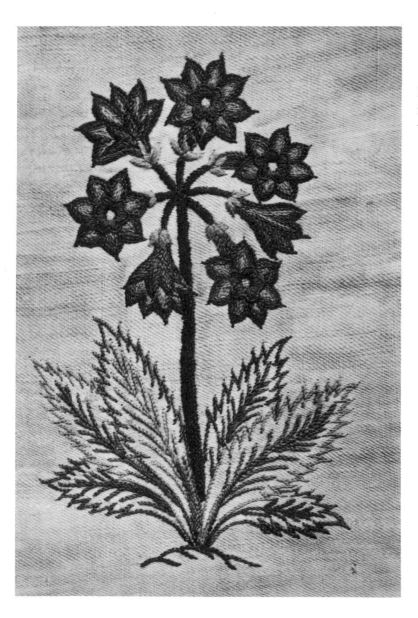

Detail from an 18th century bed hanging, in the Victoria and Albert Museum, worked in shades of rose.

This owl worked on burlap in Fishbone, Satin and Weaving Stitches shows how the technique may be adapted to a design on a bold scale.

Detail from the Abigail Pett bed, showing a wide variety of open fillings, contrasted with the solid leaves worked in Long and Short Stitch.

Designs for Individual Projects

DOWN-TO-EARTH FACTS TO HELP YOUR DESIGNS

1) *Enlarging Ready-made Designs*

A. BY PHOTOSTATIC REPRODUCTION

If you have a small photograph or drawing of the pattern you want to use you can have it enlarged photostatically. Most towns have a photostatic service, and it is an inexpensive and simple method of making a design larger or smaller. Don't try to give exact all round measurements of the finished size you need. Just measure along one side and the rest will follow naturally. Using clear tracing paper, trace the finished photograph. Both the negative and the positive will be returned to you, so you can choose which is best, but the negative is often clearer.

B. ENLARGING BY SQUARING THE DESIGN

This method is certainly one of the most ancient, but still simple and useful today. It was quaintly but clearly described by Richard Schorleyker in "A Schole House for the Needle" mentioned in the Introduction. He says, "I would have you knowe, that the use of these squares doth showe how you may contrive to worke any Bird, Beast or Flower into biger or lesser proportions, according as you shall see cause: As thus, if you will enlarge your patterne, devide it into squares, then rule a paper as large as ye list, into what squares you will: Then looke how many holes your patterne doth containe, upon so many holes of your ruled paper drawe your patterne." In case the seventeenth century English is too much for you, the illustration opposite will make things clear!

First square your design, as shown; then take a piece of paper the size the enlargement is to be, and fold it into the same number of squares (this is easier than measuring). Then draw your design to fit within them.

2) *Using Layout Paper to Make Your Own Designs*

As already mentioned in the design for the sampler (page 34) layout paper is ideal to use for making a design. First of all, it is heavy enough to be able to use afterwards for any method of transferring the design to material. Secondly, it is transparent enough to be able to trace through, without constantly erasing, which encourages sureness of line and free style. Therefore if you have a design you want to adapt, trace it first onto a sheet of layout paper, then trace it again and again, using a soft pencil, until it is satisfactory, rather than laboring on one sheet of paper. It's a good idea always to determine the outline of your finished project first, then fold the paper in four so that you have the center lines clearly defined. Then you will never find you have left too much space at the top, or too little on one side, etc. This folding idea is useful when you are making a repeat pattern too. You need only draw one section. Then fold the paper (not more than three times, or it will be too thick) and prick right through all the thicknesses. (See page 38.) This will make the repeat far more accurate than tracing several times.

Introduction to the Stitches

GENERAL NOTES

When beginning a piece of Crewel Embroidery, pick out the shapes which are half covered or which lie under the others, and work these first. For instance, sometimes a stem runs up behind a flower, then the stem should be done first. When a stem runs right up through a leaf, then the *leaf* should be worked first. In this way the shapes which lie on top may be worked so that they really overlap the others, making a clear cut line, with no chance of any material showing through at the joint.

To give your work a crisp and defined look, always exaggerate points; make them sharp by extending the stitches a little beyond the outline indicated. In the same way, when outlining, correct your embroidery to conform to the drawing by either covering or extending beyond the previous stitches.

A contemporary version of the Tree of Life design. The back of the chair was worked as the chair stands in the room where this would show.

Bedspread worked in squares and joined together with piping.

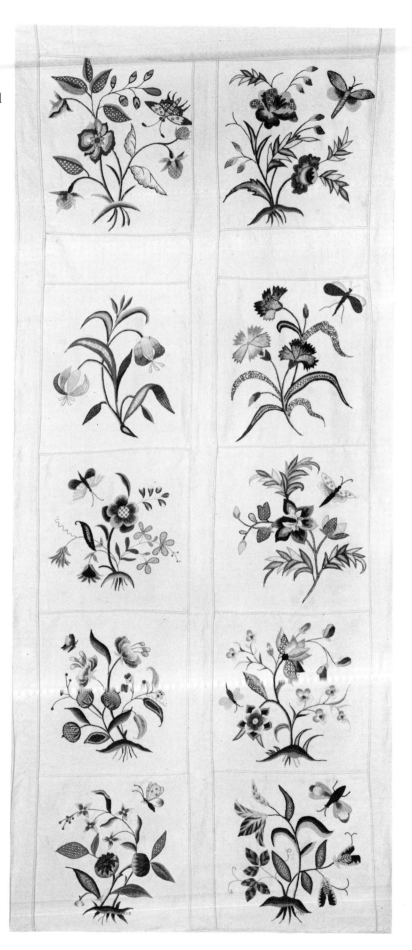

A bell-pull worked with light open stitches in the leaves and a solid stem to give continuity to the design.

Introduction to the Stitches

Many stitches can be worked either in the hand or on a frame, which-ever is preferred. Those stitches for which a frame is really essential are marked with an asterisk.

When the work is stretched tightly on a frame, the needle must always be stabbed straight up and down, never sewn. In order to make the diagrams of certain stitches clearer, the needle sometimes had to be shown *sewing* through the material. When this is the case, simply stab up and down at the letters indicated.

When working on a frame, be sure to hold the needle near the point, to control it better.

Put it in and bring it up really vertically, never on a slant. Then your stitches will be more accurate.

When there seems nowhere to end off your thread – every surround-ing line is covered – tuck the two back stitches *under* the nearest worked stitches. Pull the thread quite tight and it will never show.

Most of the stitches are equally good worked either with single or double thread. A few, however, really look best when worked with two or more threads. They are the following:

Coral, Rope, Braid, French and Bullion Knots, Turkey Work, Couch-ing, Cloud Filling (base), Knotted Pearl Stitch, Weaving Stitch.

Generally speaking, also, Satin Stitch is easier to make when it is worked with single thread. These rules only hold true for a normal effect, however, and for a larger or smaller scale any desired number of threads may be used.

Threading the Needle

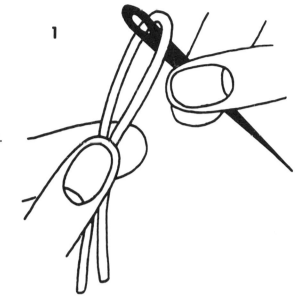

1

Wrap thread round the needle as shown.

2

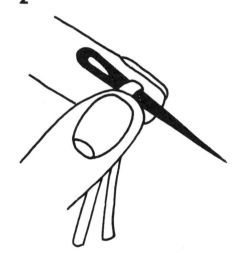

Hold thread tightly, close round needle; pull needle away.

3

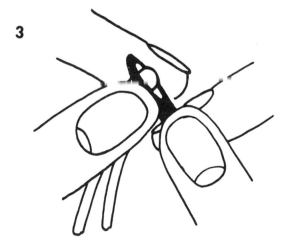

Squeeze thread *tightly* between finger and thumb, so that thread is almost buried. Press eye of needle flat down on to it. (Push the needle down on to the thread, rather than attempting to push the thread through the needle.) Pull through when amount of thread shown in diagram has appeared.

Starting and Ending Off

1

Put a knot in the thread and start on the wrong side of the material. As crewel work should always be backed, the wrong side is not of such tremendous importance, though care should be taken to keep the stitches flat, and not to jump too far from place to place without taking a small stitch in between (to prevent leaving a long loose thread on the wrong side).

2

B A

End off with 2 small back stitches on an outline or inside the shape of a design which will later be covered. (The stitches in the diagram are enlarged to show clearly – they should be very small.) Come up at A and pull through at B, then bring thread to front of work near by and cut off.

Like their name, these stitches make continuous lines and are useful worked either singly or in close rows to completely fill an area.

These flowers show how effective a design can be which is worked mainly in one or two simple stitches, in this case Satin and Stem.

Here all the outlines are worked in Coral Stitch.

Chain Stitch

Chain Stitch may be used as a solid filling, working row upon row closely side by side. Do not pack the stitches *too* closely, however, or the effect will be lost. The filling is equally effective if the lines are shaded, or worked all in one color with contrasting outline. (The stitches should all begin at the same end and run in the same direction to make a smooth effect). When extra lines have to be added to broaden the shape in one place, add them on the inside, allowing a continuous line to run along the edges. In this way the joining lines will not be obvious, especially if the first stitch of the joining line is tucked *underneath* the longer line.

Chain Stitch may also be used as an outline where a fairly broad dominant edge is needed.

Bring needle up at A.

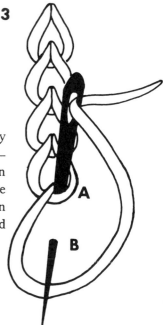

Form a loop, and put the needle in at A again, holding loop down with finger. Then come up at B, directly below A. Draw gently through, forming the first chain stitch.

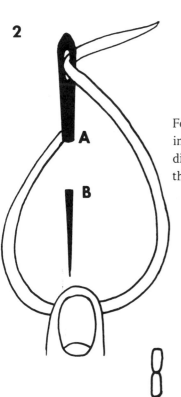

Repeat # 2, always inserting needle exactly where the thread came out, *inside* the last loop – come up directly below, and draw through so chain stitches lie flat on material. When filling a shape by working rows of Chain Stitch, always work in same direction, beginning each new row at top and working down.

Wrong side

Stem Stitch

An excellent outline stitch, Stem Stitch may also be used as a solid filling. In this case, like Chain Stitch, the lines should all be worked in the same direction for smoothness. The thread may be held either to the right or left of the needle, but once a line or a block of stitches is begun it should be held always to the same side. When working outlining, hold the thread away from the shape and towards the outside of curves. This will make the outline "roll" outwards instead of falling inwards and becoming "spikey".

When working stems and branches, work the main stem right through first, from top to bottom. Then, starting at the tips of the subsidiary stems, work them down to join the main stem, continuing the line alongside for several stitches to make a smooth join. Shorten the stitches slightly when working curves.

1

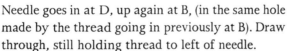

2

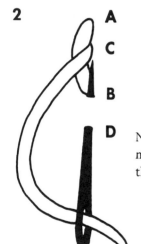

Needle comes up at A, goes in at B, and up again at C, exactly half way between A and B. Draw through, holding the thread to the left of the needle.

Needle goes in at D, up again at B, (in the same hole made by the thread going in previously at B). Draw through, still holding thread to left of needle.

3

Continue by repeating #2. The thread may be held either to the right or the left of the needle, but should remain on the same side once the work is started.

Wrong side

*Split Stitch

Like Stem and Chain Stitch, Split Stitch may be worked in close lines all in one direction. It is especially effective worked in one color when the only interest lies in the direction of line. It may be used as an outline stitch but it is more useful as an underlying padding on an edge which will later be covered with other stitching.

1

Needle comes up at A, goes down at B.

2

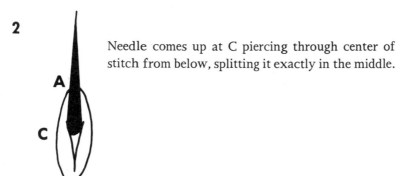

Needle comes up at C piercing through center of stitch from below, splitting it exactly in the middle.

Needle goes down at D, a little ahead of B—(the distance from C to D is the same as the length of the first stitch; from A to B.) Repeat in this way, forming a smooth line of stitching slightly shortening the stitches when going around curves.

3

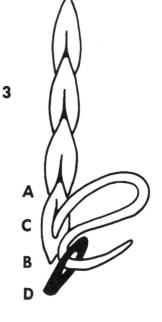

Buttonhole Stitch

This is one of the most versatile of stitches. It may be worked in solid rows, or radiating from one central point to form a circle, in scallops, or with the spokes outwards as an outline around a shape. (This was frequently used in Jacobean embroidery to soften the edge of large leaves). Always space the stitches just far enough apart to allow the loops at the edge to lie smoothly. Like Chain Stitch, Buttonhole Stitch is the basis for many other stitches, notably Coral Stitch.

1

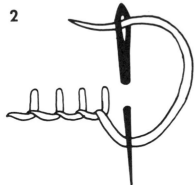

Needle comes up at A, goes in at B, and up at C directly below B, and level with A. Thread is held under needle as in diagram. Draw through downwards.

2

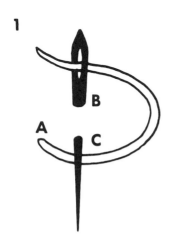

Next stitch repeats #1 at an even distance apart. Stitching may be spaced as shown, or worked closely as in #3.

3

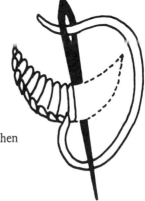

Diagram shows angle of needle when working curved shapes.

Coral Stitch

The knots may be spaced closely or far apart, but should always be at right angles to the line. When several rows are worked close together the stitches should be fitted into the spaces between the knots on the previous lines. The effect of the stitching when it is solid is almost like rows of fat French Knots. To make it effective it is best to use double thread.

1

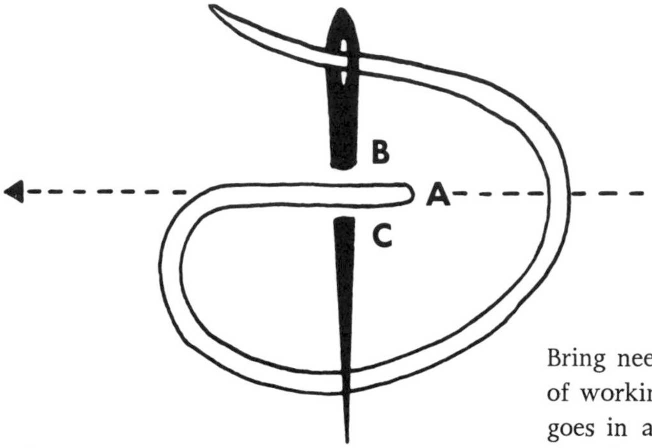

Bring needle up at A, lay thread flat in direction of working (indicated by dotted line.) Needle then goes in at B, and up at C at right angles to the thread. Holding the thread under needle (as in diagram), draw through and pull gently up to form a knot. The space between B and C determines the size of the knot.

2

Next stitch repeats #1 a little distance away. (The stitch is more effective if the knots are fairly close together).

Wrong side

Braid stitch is strictly an outline stitch, as it would be difficult to work rows close together without the needle interfering with the previous row. Single thread may be used, but double thread will show the stitch to its best advantage.

1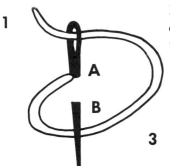

Make a small Chain Stitch. Come up at A, and go down again at A, holding the loop open—come up inside this loop at B and draw flat.

2

Anchor this Chain Stitch by going down outside the loop at C.

3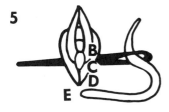

Using a blunt needle, come up at D and slide through the Chain Stitch (not through the material) from right to left (as shown).

4

Then go down at D through the material.

5

Next come up at E, just below D. Slide the needle from right to left under the anchoring stitch B-C, as well as the last chain just completed (diagram #4). Do not go through material.

6

Go down through the material at E.

7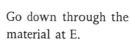

Come up at F and going back two stitches, slide the needle from right to left under both of them (as shown).

8

Continue in this way, sliding the needle from right to left under the two previous stitches together. Go down into the material where the thread came up, and come up again below ready to repeat.

9

The finished effect, drawn closely, is like a braid on top of the fabric.

Rope Stitch (narrow)

This stitch may be used as an outline, or as a solid filling, working the rows close together, all in the same direction. It is difficult to make this stitch smooth without practicing a little first, but it helps if the stitches are fairly long. Use double thread.

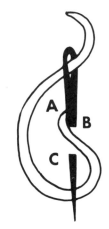

1

Come up at A and go down at B, immediately below A. Form a loop and come up at C, directly below B and inside the loop; draw flat. This stitch is like Chain, except that the thread is crossed in front of the needle before looping under it, and exactly like Rope Stitch – Broad, except that the needle is almost straight, instead of slanting.

2

Go down at D, pushing the needle very close up into the waist formed by the twisted chain. Looping the thread under the needle, come up at E on a straight line below A; draw flat.

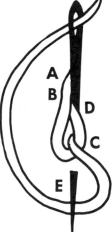

3

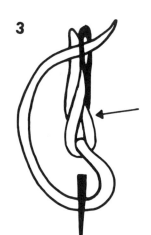

Repeat #2, and continue along the line. A smooth effect will be gained only if the needle is pushed very close, almost under the stitches (at arrow). The stitch must also be pulled down toward you to tighten it, or the loop will not lie flat.

4

Finished effect

Rope Stitch (broad)

This stitch is really exactly like Narrow Rope Stitch, except that the position of the needle is different. Used for a stem, Broad Rope appears rather like a Slanting Satin Stitch band, flat on one side and raised on the other. It may be worked as a solid filling, or a line of rope may be worked sometimes broad and sometimes narrow in one continuous line.

1

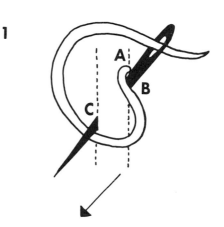

Come up at A and go down at B, tucking the needle just under A (as shown). Bring the needle out at C, twisting the thread first over and across the needle, then under it (as shown). Draw flat, pulling the thread taut in the direction of the arrow. The slant of the needle from B to C is about 45°.

2

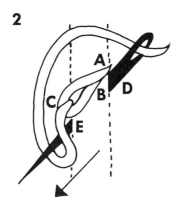

Go in at D, and come up at E, parallel with, and just touching A-C. Twist the thread over and then under the needle as before, and draw it flat, taking care not to let the loop rise up before the thread is tight. It is very easy to lose the slant and flatten out when working this stitch. To maintain the 45° angle keep the needle at D very close and touching A. Come up at E a *slight* distance below C; and again draw flat in the direction of the arrow to keep the loops lying smooth.

3

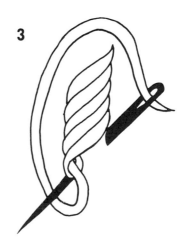

If the angle is maintained, a smooth Satin Stitch effect will result (as in diagram).

*Couching

Couching may be worked as a plain outline, having the couching threads the same color as those underneath. Either one or two threads may be used in the needle and any number of threads may be couched down. Or two contrasting colors may be used, and the top stitches worked to form patterns. Couching may be used as a solid filling, working the threads back and forth or round in circles, or following the shape of the motif being filled. It may also be used as an open filling, called Random Couching, and is worked in any direction until the ground is evenly but lightly filled.

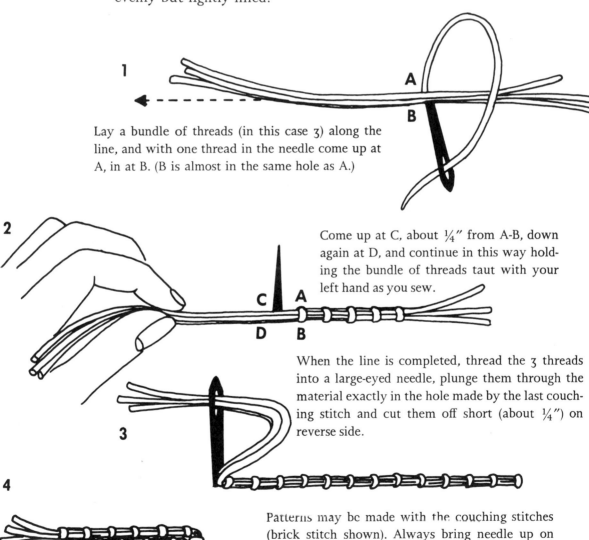

1

Lay a bundle of threads (in this case 3) along the line, and with one thread in the needle come up at A, in at B. (B is almost in the same hole as A.)

2

Come up at C, about ¼″ from A-B, down again at D, and continue in this way holding the bundle of threads taut with your left hand as you sew.

When the line is completed, thread the 3 threads into a large-eyed needle, plunge them through the material exactly in the hole made by the last couching stitch and cut them off short (about ¼″) on reverse side.

3

4

Patterns may be made with the couching stitches (brick stitch shown). Always bring needle up on the outside, and go down close to the line already worked, so that no material shows between lines of couching. At the corners work couching stitch at the angle shown to make a sharp corner without having to plunge threads at the end of each line.

Rosette Chain Stitch

It is best worked fairly small and closely, too large a stitch can easily become caught and pull when in use. It is most effective as a single line or edging.

1

Working on a line from right to left, using a blunt needle, come up at A, go down at B, a little to the left and below A, and come up at C, slightly to the right and below B. Hold the thread across in front of the needle, then twist it under the needle, as shown. Pull through, keeping the stitch lying flat on the material.

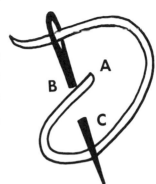

2

Now slide needle under the stitch at A, as shown. Do not pass through the material.

3

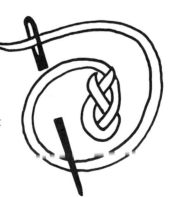

Then repeat #1, a little distance away from the stitch just made, but level with it.

4

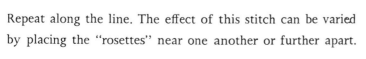

Repeat along the line. The effect of this stitch can be varied by placing the "rosettes" near one another or further apart.

Zig-zag Chain Stitch

Like Interlaced Running, this stitch needs space to show it to its best advantage.

This stitch is exactly like Chain Stitch, except that every stitch is worked at an angle to the previous one, as shown. The angle may be increased or decreased according to the effect required.

These stitches might also be called broad line stitches for they make bands which may be worked singly or in lines close together to fill an area.

Roumanian Stitch

Roumanian Stitch is really a straight Satin Stitch tied down with a smaller slanting stitch in the center. If the small stitch maintains its slant well, the stitches will fit closely together with no separation between them, keeping the effect smooth. However, this small stitch may be worked on a greater slant if the area to be filled is wide. When several bands are worked side by side the stitches should just overlap one another at the edge. If each row fits into the *exact* holes of the previous one, the stitches are apt to pull away a little and leave material showing in between.

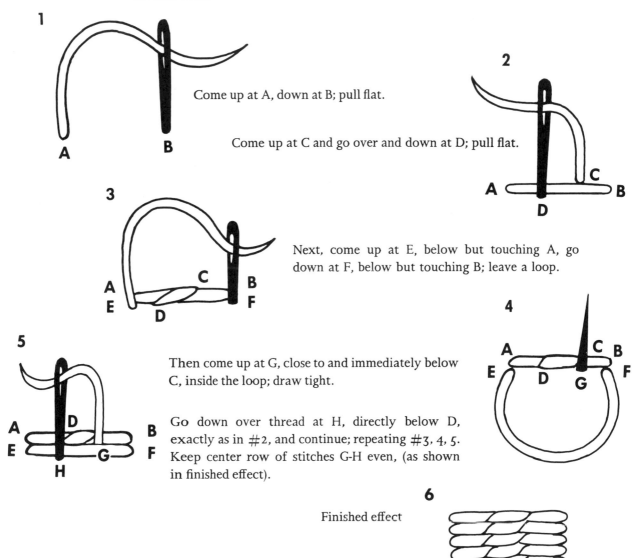

1 Come up at A, down at B; pull flat.

2 Come up at C and go over and down at D; pull flat.

3 Next, come up at E, below but touching A, go down at F, below but touching B; leave a loop.

5 Then come up at G, close to and immediately below C, inside the loop; draw tight.

Go down over thread at H, directly below D, exactly as in #2, and continue; repeating #3, 4, 5. Keep center row of stitches G-H even, (as shown in finished effect).

6 Finished effect

Cretan Stitch

This stitch may be worked very close and slanting, as shown, or flatter and with spaces between the stitches. In this way two completely different effects may be obtained, just as in Fishbone Stitch.

1

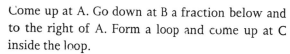

Come up at A. Go down at B a fraction below and to the right of A. Form a loop and come up at C inside the loop.

2

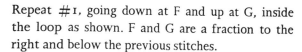

Go down at D, a fraction to the left and below A. Form a loop and come up at E, inside the loop. E is a little to the left and below C.

3

Repeat #1, going down at F and up at G, inside the loop as shown. F and G are a fraction to the right and below the previous stitches.

4

Repeat #2. Needle goes down and comes up a fraction to the left and below other stitches, coming up inside the loop each time.

5

Continue in this way so that a plait is formed down the center of the shape. Keep the stitches very close together on the edge to maintain the slant, and the center stitches on an even line below one another, as shown.

6

Finished effect

Van Dyke Stitch

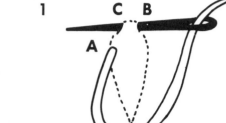

Using a blunt needle, come up at A and take a small stitch from B to C at top of shape to be worked (as shown).

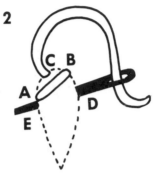

Go down at D and up at E, a needle's width below A on the outline.

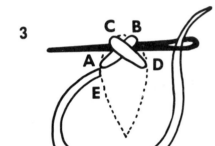

Slide needle from right to left under the Cross Stitch formed by A-B, and C-D. Do not go through the material.

Go down at F on the outline, a needle's width below D. Come up at G below E on the outline.

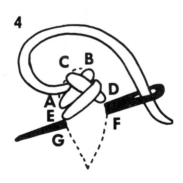

Repeat #3 and #4 until shape is filled. If the tension is even (do not pull too tightly), a raised braid will be formed smoothly down the center.

Knotted Pearl Stitch

The Buttonhole Stitches should not be pulled too tight, and should always be drawn up into the center of the band, to make a row of raised knots down the middle of the stitch. Do not attempt to work too wide a band with it.

1

Come up at A, go down at B, and up again at C. A-B-C are all on a straight line (as shown).

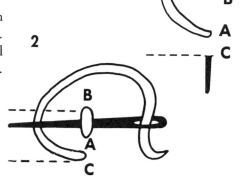

2

Using a blunt needle, slide under stitch B-A from right to left without going through material. Holding loop under the needle (as shown), pull flat. This forms one Buttonhole Stitch on bar B-A.

3

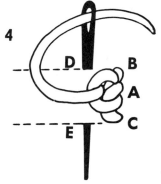

Now work a second Buttonhole Stitch by going under the bar B-A again, exactly as in #2.

4

Go down through the material at D, come up at E. D and E are level with B and C (as shown).

5

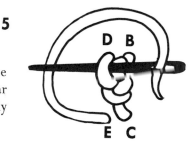

Now repeat procedure of #2 again . . . this time the Buttonhole Stitches are worked into the bar at D (as shown). Be very careful to pick up only the bar at D and not the other stitches.

6

Finished effect. To complete row, go down outside last Buttonhole loop to anchor it.

Herringbone Stitch

This stitch is the simple foundation for many variations. It may be worked as broad or narrow as desired and may require a little practice at first to keep it regularly spaced and even.

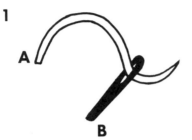

Come up at A, go down at B, diagonally below A.

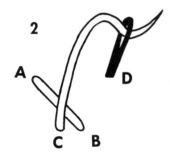

Come up at C, a little to the left, and level with B, and go down at D, level with A, making a diagonal stitch in the other direction.

Come up at E, a little to the left and level with D, go down at F. E to F is another diagonal stitch parallel with A-B. Repeat from #2 again.

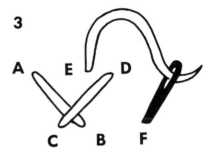

Continue repeating #2 and #3, spacing the stitches evenly so that the diagonals are parallel.

Close Herringbone Stitch

This stitch is smoothest if kept slanting. Space the stitches a little apart when the needle goes down, and keep them close together (almost touching) when the needle comes up on the edge. This will help maintain the slant, and make a sharp V in the center. It is attractive when used on small leaves.

1

Come up at A, go down at B, diagonally below A.

2

Come up at C, go down at D (C is directly below A; D is directly above B).

Come up at E, close to A, go down at F, close to B.

3

4

Come up at G, close to C, go down at H close to D.

Continue in this way along the line, forming a solid band of stitching.

5

6

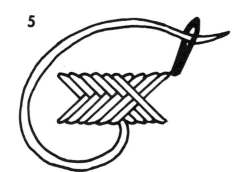

To work a shape as above, start exactly on point A and work in direction of B, coming up and down on outline so that stitches automatically fill the shape.

Fishbone Stitch

The first stitch (A to B) should be at least ¼″ long to start the stitch off on a good slant. To maintain this slant, bring the needle up and go down on the edge, almost in the same holes as the previous stitches, and keep the center stitch (B to E) a good length. The stitch looks best if a smooth edge is made which does not need outlining afterwards. Like Cretan, Fishbone may also be worked with spaces between the stitches for an open effect.

1

Come up at A in the center of point. Go down at B directly below it—(draw line down center as guide line.) Come up at C to left and slightly below A, but touching it, on outline of shape.

Go in at D to right and slightly below A, but touching it. Come up at B, and form a loop by holding thread under needle.

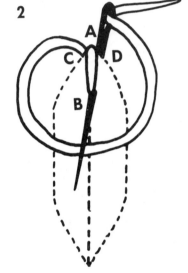

2

3

Draw through and insert needle at E a short space directly below B, come up at F—again to the left and slightly below C, but touching it.

4

Now repeat #2 again; come up at F, go in at G (touching previous threads). Come up at E with thread under the needle. Anchor it down as in #3, and continue in this way.

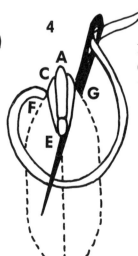

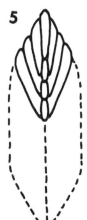

5

Finished effect.

Raised Stem Stitch*

Though it is shown here as a banding stitch, Raised Stem may be used to fill whole areas. In this case the long basic stitches should be tacked down invisibly here and there, afterwards. The stitch may be shaded, working in vertical bands, or stripes of contrasting colors. When used to fill an uneven area it usually needs an outline of Stem Stitch.

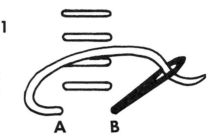

First work a series of parallel stitches (just under ¼" apart, as shown in diagram). To work a wider area than the one shown, lay these lines across the whole width of the shape.

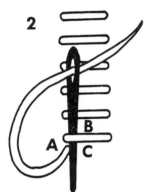

Using a blunt (tapestry) needle, come up at A, and holding thread to left of needle slide under first thread from B to C. Do not go through material.

Repeat #2, sliding needle under thread from D to E, and work up to top of thread in this way.

Work several lines close side by side always beginning again at the bottom, working upwards until base threads are entirely covered. Do not pack too many rows in, however, or the effect will be lost.

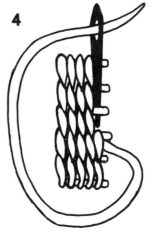

*Raised Chain Stitch

See notes on Raised Stem Stitch.

102   **1**

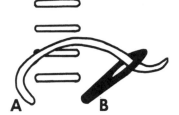

First work a series of parallel stitches (just under ¼″ apart) as shown in diagram. (As for Raised Stem Stitch.)

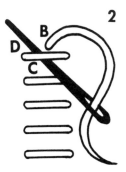

2

Then bring thread up at B and slide under thread from C to D (do not go through material). This stitch is best worked with a blunt needle. Draw through and hold thread upwards keeping it rather taut.

3

Next slide needle downwards under same thread, but to the right of first stitch, from E to F, draw through, holding thread under needle; do not pull too tightly so the appearance of the stitch is as in #4.

4

Continue stitch by repeating #2 and #3. Several rows may be worked side by side to fill a space (as in Raised Stem Stitch) instead of single row shown. In this case end off row at base and start again at the top, ready to work downwards.

Raised Buttonhole Stitch[*]

See notes on Raised Stem Stitch.

1

First lay a series of parallel stitches just under ¼″ apart (as shown in diagram).

2

Using a blunt needle, come up at A, form a loop with the thread, and without going through the material, slide under the first bar from B to C (as shown). Draw down towards you until the thread is snug. This forms a Buttonhole Stitch on the horizontal bar.

3

Repeat #2, sliding the needle under the thread from D to E, and work to the bottom of the bars in this way. When you have reached the bottom of each line, anchor the final stitch by going down through the material over the buttonhole loop at F (as in diagram #4).

4

Work several lines close side by side, always beginning at the top, working downwards, until the bars are entirely covered. Do not pack too many rows in or the effect will be lost.

Solid Filling Stitches

Like their name, these stitches may be used to fill areas with close stitches, leaving no material showing through.

Slanting Satin Stitch*

This stitch needs practice in order to make it neat and even. The slant helps to make it smoother, and the Split Stitch padding makes it easier to keep the edge clean; both essential to the effect. It should never be used for large areas, because the threads could easily be pulled and disarranged when the embroidery is in use. On very small leaves it is easier to start at the tip and work downwards. To maintain the slant, come up close at the upper edge and go down with a slight space between the stitches on the lower edge. This tends to exaggerate the slant of each stitch but prevents them from flattening out.

1

First outline shape with Split Stitch.

2

Starting in the center (to be certain of the exact angle), work slanting stitches close together across the shape, coming up and going down outside the Split Stitch. (Split Stitch forms a padding on the outline, giving a firm edge.)

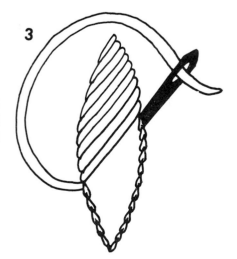

3

Work up to tip, then start at center again and finish working shape to the bottom. Stitches should lie evenly side by side, not crowded, but no material showing between. Do not pull too tightly.

*Satin Stitch — Tied with Back Stitch

This stitch may be used to fill a wider area, for unlike Slanting Satin Stitch, it has a row of stitching to hold it in the center. More than one row of Back Stitch may be worked if the area needs it. Do not pull the Back Stitch too tight for it will spoil the evenness of the Satin Stitch underneath it.

Having outlined shape with Split Stitch, Satin Stitch over it, starting in center to guide stitches at the correct angle. Keep stitches fairly upright at outside points (as shown). It is easier to work longer stitches instead of very short ones.

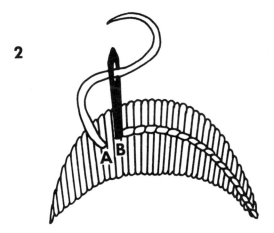

As stitches would be too long to leave untied, work a row of Back Stitch through the center of the shape, using the upper edge as a guide line. Needle comes up at A, and down at B, right into the hole made by the last stitch.

Padded Satin Stitch *

The top row of Padded Satin Stitch may be worked straight instead of slanting, but this is much harder to make even, especially when the stitches are small at the point of a leaf. It is therefore best to practice it on a slant first.

1

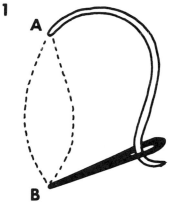

Starting in the center of the shape, come up at A, down at B.

2

Fill shape with stitches just side by side.

3

Go across with a few stitches to hold the long ones flat.

4

For the second padding, go up and down vertically again as in #2.

Come up at A, down at B, and cover the whole shape with slanting stitches as shown. To maintain the slant, A should always be a fraction ahead of the last stitch, and B should be pushed up very close to the previous stitches. (Otherwise the slant becomes flatter and flatter until it is almost straight.)

5

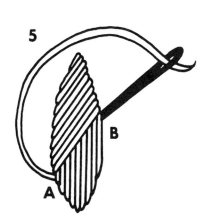

*Block Shading

Like Roumanian Stitch, bands of Block Shading should fit closely together, slightly overlapping the previous row, to prevent any material showing between them. When used to fill shapes, Block Shading should have the same direction of stitch as Long and Short. (See diagram page 114.) It is advisable to mark this direction in pencil on the material before working. Never outline Block Shading afterwards, the edge will be smooth and raised because of the Split Stitch padding.

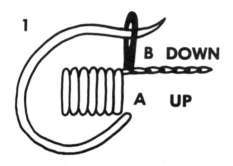

1

First outline shape to be worked with Split Stitch. Then work a row of Satin Stitches, bringing needle up at A, down at B, over Split Stitch. (This makes a firm, even edge.) Keep all the stitches close and even, side by side.

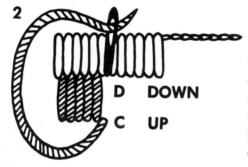

2

Using the next shade, work a second row, repeating the first exactly. Come up at C, down at D, just between the stitches of the previous row. Block shading consists of even bands of Satin Stitches, changing color with each row, but showing a clear division between each band.

3

To work round a curve, place the stitches slightly wider apart on the edge, closer in the center to fan them, leaving no visible space between them, however. Occasionally slip in a shorter wedge stitch to help fan them (as shown in the diagram by the arrow).

Long and Short Stitch — Tapestry Shading*

Whole designs, including the background, may be worked in Tapestry Shading. The effect will be like its name; the vertical shading of tapestry. This is a good stitch to practice before trying Long and Short – Soft Shading, since you can experiment with the size of the stitch and correct blending of the colors without having to bother about changing direction. Use double thread for practicing so that the stitches are clear. Though the colors should blend, it is better to have a clearly defined difference between them to show the stitch to its best advantage. In spite of the difference in length of the stitches, the rows should be as regular and definite as those in Block Shading. An outline afterwards will spoil the effect of the raised edge obtained by the Split Stitch padding.

First work a row of Split Stitch along the outline. This stitch will be covered by Long and Short, but it is valuable as a firm padding and enables you to make a knife-sharp edge with the Long and Short. Come up at A and go down at B just *over* Split Stitch. Work a row of Long and Short Stitches side by side, as in diagram. (The short stitch is ¾ of the length of the long one.) Keep each long stitch alike and all the short stitches the same length.

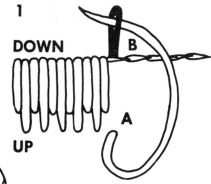

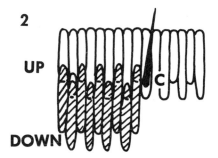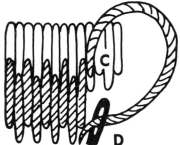

Next row. In another shade, *split up* through the first long and short stitches ¼ of the way back, at C. Go down into the material at D. These stitches are all of equal length, but are staggered in brick fashion to fit up into the long and short previous row. The dotted line on diagram shows how much of each previous stitch lies under the succeeding row.

In a third color, work a third line of stitches the same way (repeating #2), always coming up ¼ of the way back through the stitch. Be sure each row is long enough. Remember ¼ of the stitch will be obscured when the succeeding row is worked into it, and allow for this. Any number of rows may be worked in this way, using any number of colors, or only one. The best effect is obtained, however, if the rows are shaded gradually from dark to light, or light to dark, as in diagram.

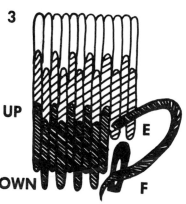

* Long and Short – Soft Shading

GENERAL RULES TO REMEMBER FOR LONG AND SHORT STITCH

110

1. FIRST ROW. Come up inside the shape, go *down* over Split Stitch to make a good outline.

2. SECOND ROW. Split *up* through the stitches of the first row, and go *down* into the material, to make a smooth blending of color where the first and second rows join. Repeat #2 on succeeding rows.

3. Keep *all* the rows long enough to allow the subsequent stitches to split back into them.

4. Start at the tip or furthest from the growing point of flowers, fruits, or leaves, then work down towards the growing point in order to keep stitches flowing smoothly.

5. Do not change direction abruptly; always let the stitches flow gradually and smoothly from one row to another, changing direction imperceptibly if necessary.

6. When working shapes which overlap one another, work the underneath one first, then Split Stitch and work the next overlapping one, and repeat.

7. If at first you don't succeed, don't be discouraged, but try, try again!

Long and Short – Soft Shading repeats the principle of Tapestry Shading exactly. Instead of running straight up and down, however, the stitches follow direction lines as indicated in the diagram, Direction of Stitches for Long and Short.

First draw guide lines in pencil on the material (as shown by dotted lines). Then outline the shape with Split Stitch, both the inner ring and outer petals. Next work the first row of Long and Short, coming up at A and going down *over* the Split Stitch at B, starting in the center (or highest point) of each petal. It is easier to work downwards from the center on either side, since the angle of the stitch is straight to begin with, then gradually fans very slightly on each side. To achieve this, the stitches may be placed slightly wider apart on the outside edge and closer in the center, exactly like a fan. If this is not sufficient, a greater slant may be obtained by taking an extra short stitch over the upper edge occasionally (as indicated by the arrow in the diagram). This "wedge stitch" will not show, providing the next stitch is taken extremely close to it. On the shape illustrated, few wedge stitches are necessary since all the stitches gravitate to the center of the flower like the spokes of a wheel.

1

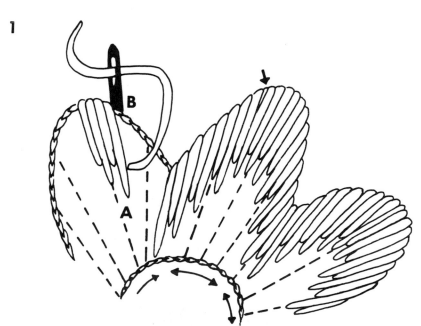

2

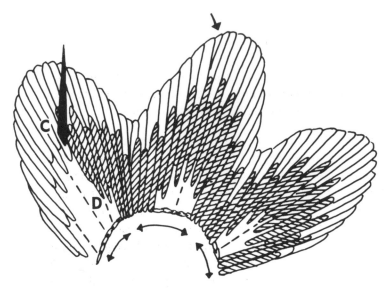

Work a second row of stitches in the next shade lighter or darker, coming up at C and down at D. Here again the stitches fan slightly as in the first row. They should not change direction abruptly, but should flow into one another smoothly. As in Tapestry Shading, be sure to split far enough back into the previous row and make the stitches long enough for the third row to split into them.

In the shape illustrated this second row of stitches comes right over the outline at the lowest point of the petals (as shown).

With the third color, fill the remaining spaces in the center of each petal only. Come up at E and go down at F. Bring the stitches evenly down *over* the Split Stitch, making a smooth outline as at the beginning. On the third row it is impossible to fit each stitch *exactly* back through the previous stitch; every now and again miss one (as in the diagram). This is because there is less space in the center of the curve than on the outside. Still make the stitches look regular, keeping a long and short effect.

3

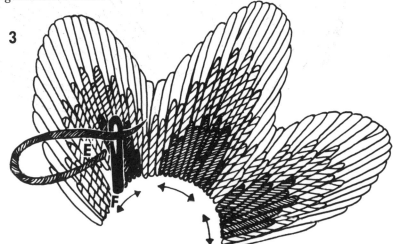

1   **2**   **3**

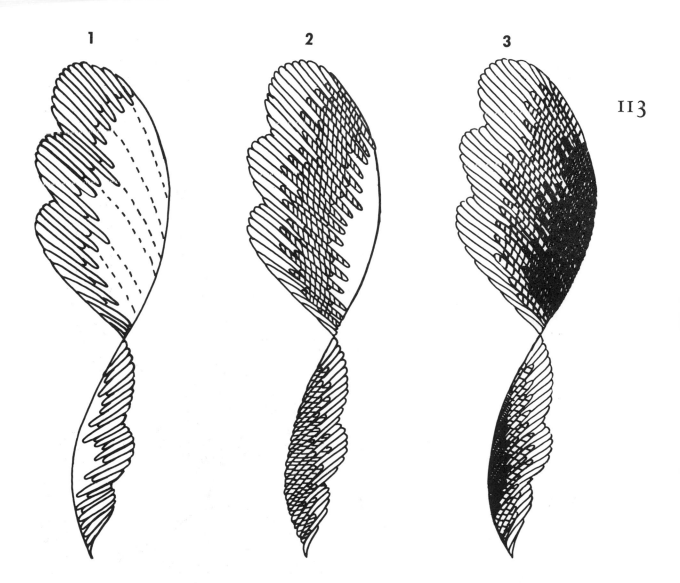

The first line (1) is a band of stitching following the outline exactly like Block Shading, but with alternate long and short stitches. Follow this with the second line (2) in the same way, being certain to take the stitches high into the first stitches and echo the outline. The third row (3) repeats the second and makes a smooth row of outline stitches on the opposite side of the leaf (as shown).

Direction of Stitches for Long and Short

114

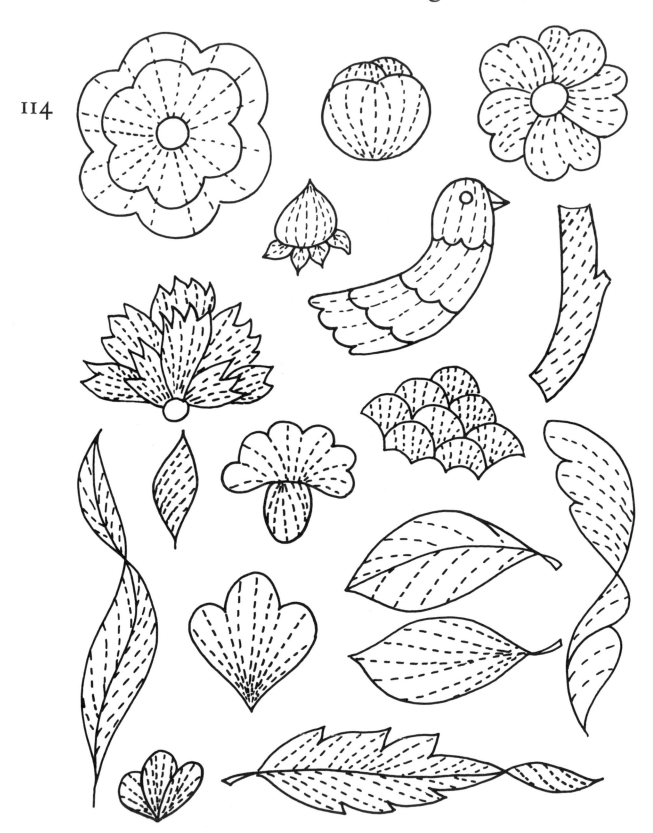

LAID WORK TIED WITH CROSS BARS—
LAID WORK TIED DIAGONALLY–SHADED LAID WORK

This is a most useful stitch for covering large areas, either in one color or several. It must be tied down afterwards, or the long threads would catch when the embroidery was in use. This tying down may be done in many ways as shown on the subsequent pages, either with criss-crossing lines, parallel lines tied down with a small tacking stitch, with Split Stitch, Coral, or practically any other line stitch. The first three are the most usual because they do not disturb the Laid Stitches underneath, but Laid Work is very versatile, and even open fillings such as Burden Stitch may be used to cover it. It is usually best to lay the lines across the longest direction of the shape but remember the tie-down stitches will predominate, and as these will run in the opposite direction to the first layer, consider this before starting. Always start laying the basic threads across the center or broadest part of the design to set the direction. Small awkward corners are then easier to fill in later. A strong outline afterwards is essential.

TIED WITH CROSS BARS

Needle comes up at A, goes in at B right across widest point of shape, to establish desired direction. All subsequent stitches are parallel to this line.

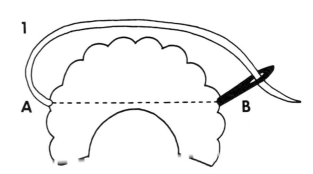

Next stitch comes up at C, close to B, and goes down again at D, close to A.

3

Continue working in this way, coming up close beneath previous stitch, on the same side as where you went down. (Stitches should lie evenly side by side with no material showing between them.) When lower half is completed go back to center and work upper half in same way.

Starting in broadest part of shape come up at A, down at B, laying a long thread diagonally across shape (angle is indicated by dotted line). This should cut across Laid Work threads at about 45°.

4

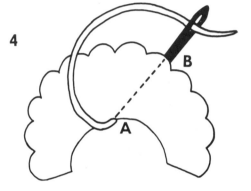

5

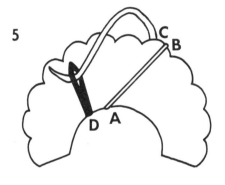

Come up at C, about ¼″ away from B, and go in at D, making a line parallel to A and B. Cover the whole shape in this way, and then work lines in the other direction to make perfect diamonds as shown in #6.

6

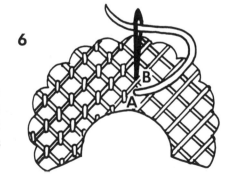

These threads are now tied down by a small stitch at each intersection. Come up at A, and go down at B, as shown, until all threads are tied down. At the edge make a little half stitch if necessary (as shown).

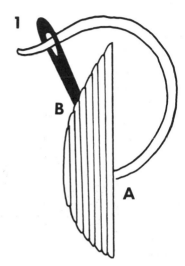

Having worked Laid Work over area (in direction shown), come up at A, down at B. This stitch lies across broadest area of the shape, to set the correct angle for the following stitches.

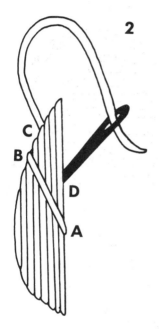

Come up at C, down at D, making a line parallel to A and B, about ¼" above it. Then work from the center downwards until whole shape is laid with parallel slanting lines.

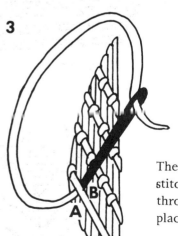

These lines must then be tied down with small stitches. Come up at A, down at B, going right through the material. These stitches should be placed alternately.

* Shaded Laid Work

1

A

B

Come up at A, and go down at B. Use the lightest color and lay a line across the shape near the upper end at right angles to the center, (indicated here by dotted line). When the shape is irregular (as here), do not start at the tip, for the correct direction of the stitches may be lost by the time the broad part of the design is reached.

Working downwards, lay two *separate* lines the width of one thread apart, (as in diagram from C to D, E to F). Then working upwards, come up at G, down at H, and continue laying lines close together to the tip.

With medium color, fill in *between* the lines A-B, C-D, and E-F, where the spaces were left. Continue downwards, laying a solid block of medium-colored stitches. Then lay two more separate lines the distance of one thread apart (as shown) like #2.

With the darkest color fill in the spaces left between the separate lines of medium color.

Continue laying dark-colored threads solidly to the bottom until the shape is covered. By spacing the lines at the end of each block of color and filling in between with the next shade, the colors blend softly.

Tie down with lines of Split Stitch. The direction of these lines depends on the shape of the design, but should be approximately at a 45° angle to the Laid Work lines.

In the case of this leaf, work a vein through the center first, then add the side veins in approximately parallel sweeping lines.

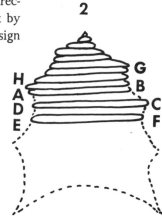

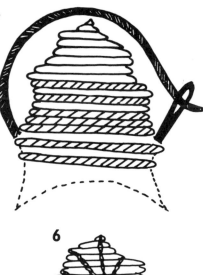

Open or Patterned Filling Stitches

Most of the open fillings included here are based on regular squares —
very good training for the eye when beginning crewel work, since learning to space the stitches evenly is most important. Generally they are
best used for bold stylized patterns.

*Burden Stitch

This stitch may be used as a filling, or to cover large background spaces. It is attractive worked either very closely so that the basic threads hardly show, or quite wide apart to make an open lacy effect. It has the advantage of being an open filling, yet one where it is very easy to change color. The finished effect is almost like weaving. Generally it is best done in double thread, using the darkest color to underlay it and outlining the finished shape all round afterwards.

1

Coming up at A, going down at B, up at C, down at D, etc., lay parallel lines about ¼″ apart (coming up the same side as you go down.)

2

Work the complete line (as shown), coming up at G and going down at H. G is immediately below and *really touching* line A-B; H is immediately above and *really touching* line E-F. Keep all stitches at right angles to the original laid lines.

3

Coming up at J, just below the line, go down at K, just above the line as in #2. Come up in between the previous stitches, fitting them in like bricks. Again take care to make stitches touch the lines above and below. The finished effect is like weaving, as though the vertical stitches disappear under the horizontal ones.

4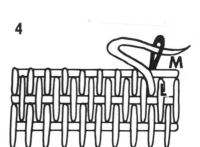

To finish the upper row, come up at L and go down at M, just over the top line. (It is easier to finish the top row of stitching after the scale has been set by the other rows.)

5

When shading use two needles and completely finish one row before going to the next. In row 3 for instance, work nearly to the center with light color, work one stitch of dark, change to light again and finish the row. In row 4 work the light stitches, then two stitches of dark and finish in light. (If all one color were worked first, insufficient space might be left for the other color, causing uneven spacing between stitches.)

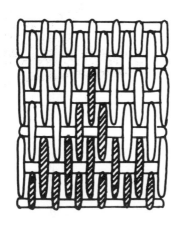

SQUARED FILLINGS # 1 TO # 10

The following are just a few of the many variations of Squared Fillings. Once you have grasped the basic idea, it is a simple matter to invent your own, and so add more to the collection. Squared Fillings are useful for breaking up plain areas, and it is possible to achieve unlimited color combinations with them. Squared Filling #3 may be shaded by changing the color in the blocks of Satin Stitch. All of them look best when used to fill stylized shapes and when combined with simple flat areas such as Laid Work in one color. They are so variegated in themselves that they need plain surroundings to set them off.

1

Coming up on one side of shape, make a long stitch right across, going down on other side. Fill the whole shape with exact parallel lines about ¼" apart.

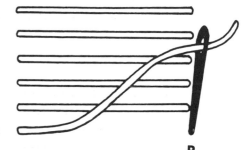

A

B

2

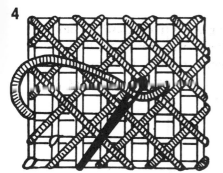

C

D

Then lay threads in the opposite direction, making perfect squares.

3

Tie down these squares at the corners with small stitches, all slanting in the same direction, as shown.

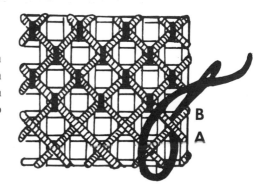

Using a contrasting color, diagonally criss-cross whole design with long lines, first in one direction across the center of every other square, then in the other direction so that the threads cross in the center of the basic squares.

4

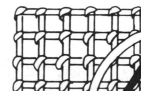

5

With another contrasting color, tie down these diagonal lines where they cross in the center of the squares. This stitch should touch the basic squares at the top and bottom.

B

A

121

*Squared Filling #2

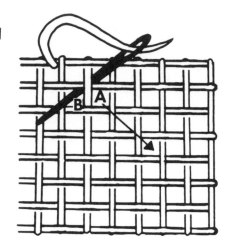

1

Use a blunt (tapestry) needle for this stitch. Having laid long, parallel lines in one direction, go across in the other direction, but instead of laying the lines on top (as in squared filling #1), weave under and over like darning, making squares as shown.

Starting across broadest part of shape, with contrasting color, pick up the first threads diagonally at intersection slipping needle through from A to B as shown. (Do not sew through the material.)

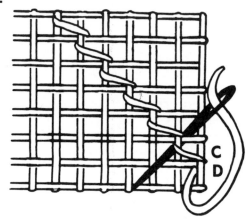

2

Work diagonally across as in diagram. Go through the material at C, and up at D, and start working upwards; take up threads at intersection exactly as when working downwards. Do not pull too tightly.

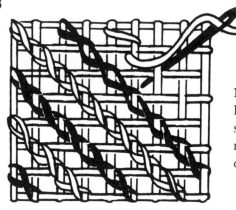

3

Now repeat #2 using another contrasting color, leaving one intersection clear between the lines of stitching. Cover the entire shape in this way, alternating lines of color and leaving one intersection clear between each line.

1

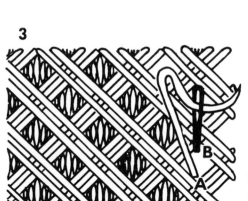

Lay parallel lines diagonally across the space to be filled, two lines close together though not touching, then a wider space, then two closer again, and so on (as shown).

2

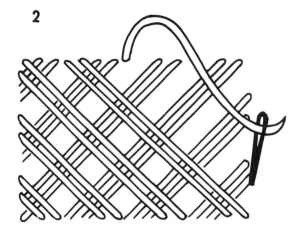

Using the same color, repeat #1 in the opposite direction to make diamonds.

3

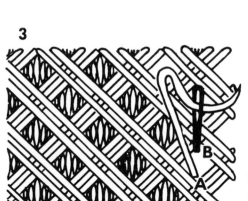

Using another color, fill each large diamond with Satin Stitch. To start the stitches evenly, put one stitch across the center, then two or three small stitches on either side.

With a third contrasting color, tie down the crisscross lines with four stitches coming up in the Satin Stitch and going down in the center, thus forming a star. When you tie down with these four stitches, be certain to maintain the space between the diagonal lines so a little material shows through (as shown).

Squared Filling #3 may be shaded by changing the color of the Satin Stitches in the diamond.

4

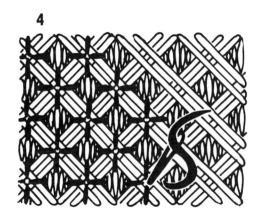

* Squared Fillings # 4 and # 5

124

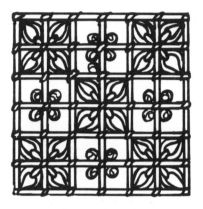

#4. Both patterns have a base of squares tied down at the corners as in Squared Filling #1. For Filling #4 work four Detached Chain Stitches converging at one point, as shown. Place them in checkerboard fashion, leaving four empty squares between each block. Then work four French Knots close together in the corners of the empty squares, using a contrasting color.

#5. Work exactly the same way as #4 but leave a clear line of squares around the blocks of Detached Chain Stitches. Then work five Slanting Satin Stitches in the blank square connecting the corners of the blocks, as shown.

#6. Start with a block of squares as in Squared Filling #1. Do not tie them down. With a blunt needle and contrasting thread, weave diagonally across the squares, picking up the *under* thread of the foundation, as shown.

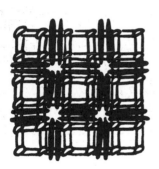

#7 and 8. First lay a foundation of squares and tie them down as in Squared Filling #1. For #7, work two stitches side by side (not touching) right over the squares, radiating them from a central square, as shown.

For #8, work a cross right over every other square, checkerboard fashion, but do not allow the crosses to touch one another.

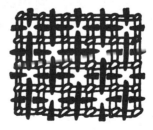

* Squared Filling # 9

Coming up on one side of shape, make a long stitch right across, going down on other side. Fill the whole shape with exact parallel lines about ¼" apart.

1

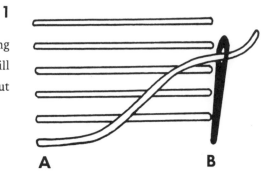

A   B

2

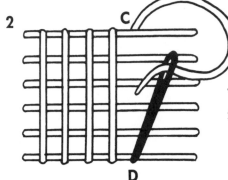

C

D

Then lay threads in the opposite direction, making perfect squares.

3

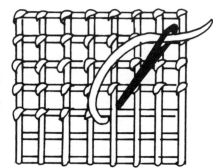

Tie down these squares at the corners with small stitches, all slanting in the same direction, as shown.

4

Using a contrasting color diagonally criss-cross the whole design with long lines, first in one direction across the center of every other square, then in the other direction, so that the threads cross exactly where the basic square threads crossed. In this way a series of stars is formed, each with eight bars radiating from the center.

5

Using a blunt needle and with another contrasting color, tie down these diagonal lines where they cross and converge with the basic squares. To do this, come up on the left of one of the "square" lines and weave round in a circle, passing over the diagonal and picking up the "square" lines as you go round. Go down through the material just on the right of where you came up. Do not pull the circle too tight or it will disappear. A strong contrast in color is needed to make it show up well.

1

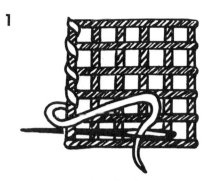

Lay basic squares as in Squared Filling #1. Do not tie them down. Starting at the top, using a blunt needle and contrasting color, whip over each thread from right to left, working down to the bottom. At the bottom of the line go down through the material to anchor the thread, come up again a fraction away, and whip up to the top on the same thread again weaving the needle under from right to left.

2

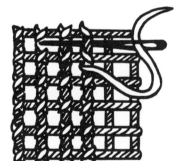

Whip over all the upright bars in this way, and then repeat exactly the same thing on the horizontal ones.

3

Finished effect. Because the thread crosses four times at the intersections, the cross effect shown in the diagram does not appear clearly. The bars simply become raised bumps where they cross.

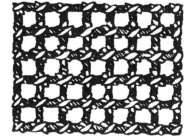

* Wave Stitch

1

Coming up at A, and going down at B, make a row of straight stitches along the top of the shape to be covered. For clarity the spacing is shown wider in the diagram than it should be when worked.

2

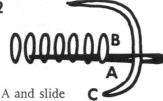

3

Using a blunt needle, come up at C in a direct line below A and slide the needle through the stitch A-B. Do not pass through the material.

Go down through material at D, close to and on a line with C, and come up at E, close to D and on a line with it. Slide through the next straight stitch above (as in 2), and repeat to the end of line.

4

Starting on the right again, come up at F, the same distance below C as C was from A. Slide the needle under C. Do not go through the material.

5

Go down at G, come up close to it at H, and slide through D and E together (not through the material).

6

Continue sliding through two stitches together to the end of the row.

7

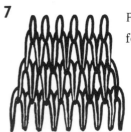

Finished effect. The stitches should be placed fairly closely, as shown, for this stitch to be really effective.

1

Work a series of straight stitches over the ground to
be covered, using a double thread and spacing them
evenly, checkerboard fashion, as shown.

2

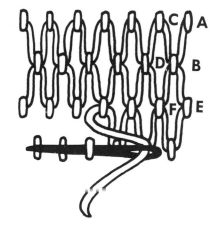

Using a contrasting color, a single thread, and a blunt
needle, thread through these straight stitches from
right to left. Begin at A, go down to B, up to C, down
to D, and so on to the end of the line.

Then start again at E on the right, go up to B, down to
F, and so on. This stitch is more effective when there
is a strong contrast either in thickness or color or
both, between the straight foundation stitches and the
interlacing thread.

Seeding

1

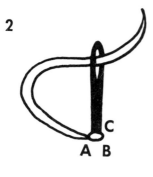

Come up at A, go down at B, a fraction away from A. Draw through, but not too tight.

2

Coming up at A, work another stitch over the first. Go down at C close to, but not in the same hole as B. This makes the stitch fatter; the finished effect should be a raised knob, almost as broad as it is long.

3

Finished effect (enlarged). Work a series of these stitches all scattered over the surface in different directions. Take care not to pull the thread too tightly.

4

Finished effect showing shading stitches closely spaced at the edge, wider in the center.

This stitch is really borrowed from the Florentine Stitch of needle-point or canvas work, but it makes an effective filling which may be carried out in as many colors as you please. It usually looks best if it is not outlined, so take care to keep the edge neat.

Lay parallel lines across shape to be worked, by coming up at A, going down at B. Lines are approximately ¼" apart. Always come up and go down on the same side of the outline, to avoid long threads on the back.

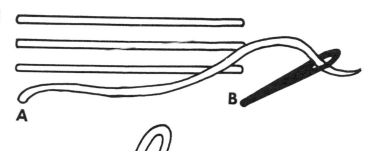

Start by coming up right underneath line #1, pass over line #2 and down close below line #3. Do four stitches in this way side by side. Now bring needle up right underneath line #2, pass over line #3, and down close below line #4. Do four stitches in this way side by side.

Now repeat this, coming up under #3, going over #4 and down just under #5. Continue these blocks of four stitches, going down three lines and up three lines until you have finished a complete row (as illustrated). Now, start over again, using a shade deeper color. Come up exactly in the hole made by the previous thread, underneath line #3, pass over line #4 and go down close below line #5. Continue in this manner across the complete row.

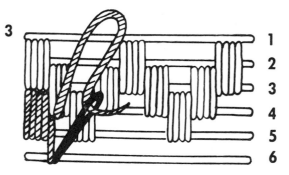

Now start your third row with a still deeper color. Then repeat the light shade, medium shade, and dark color over again (as shown in diagram). Always complete one row before beginning the next. Always start across the widest space to be filled, since the first row acts as a guide for all subsequent shorter rows.

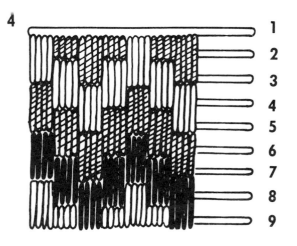

*Weaving Stitch

This is really exactly like sock darning! It may be done with at least two or three threads in both directions. Then when the weaving is completed evenly the result is a series of perfect squares in contrasting colors. It is also possible to use three or four threads for laying the first row of stitching, then to darn through with only one or two in the other direction. (This is useful to give a seeded effect on a strawberry, for instance.) Try to keep the outline even, for this stitch usually looks best if it is not outlined.

1

Come up at A, down at B, up at C, down at D, etc., laying threads side by side (the width of one thread apart).

Change to a blunt tapestry needle, and using a contrasting color, come up at M. Weave under and over the threads, starting through the center (or the widest part). Go down through the material at N.

2

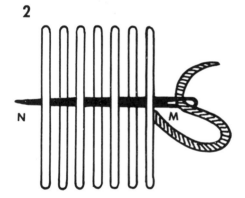

3

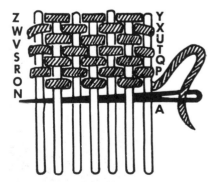

Come up through the material at O, and weave through the threads, go down at P, up at Q, continue to Z, pushing threads together so that even squares of each color are obtained. Go back to the center (A), and finish weaving the lower part.

If the loops get in the way while working, pin them down to the material. Do not be afraid to cut the loops down in the end, the result is neater if the effect is like a piece of thick velvet. It is always easier to work the stitch in rows horizontally regardless of what shape is being filled.

1

Go down at A, come up at B. Do not knot the thread, but leave about 1″ hanging on top, (as shown in diagram #2). Arrow indicates direction of working.

2

With thread *below* the needle, on a line with A and B, go down at C, and come up in same hole as A. Draw this stitch tight, holding on to the loose end of thread, (so that it does not pull right through the material).

3

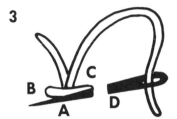

With the thread *above* the needle, go down at D, come up in the same hole as C. *Do not* draw tight, but leave a loop, (as shown). In this stitch, the needle should always be horizontal. (In order to show the stitch clearly in the diagram, it has been drawn on a slant.)

With the thread once more *below* the needle, go in at E, and up in the same hole as D; pull tight.

4

5

Continue along the line, coming up each time into the hole made by the previous stitch. The thread is alternately above the needle, leaving a loop, and below the needle drawing it tight.

Finished effect of single line. Work this stitch in lines one after the other. To achieve a thick velvety effect at the end, take small stitches and work the lines very close together. (This working diagram is much enlarged.)

6

7

Having filled the shape, cut all the loops along dotted line (as shown in diagram). Do not cut each line individually; trim the whole shape to the desired length, (a full 1/8″ long).

8

Finished effect

Composite Stitches

So called because they are worked with more than one step and often more than one color.

Interlaced Cable Chain Stitch

This stitch is useful as a single line, or it may be worked in rows and interlaced to make a light open filling as shown. When used as the latter it is more effective to use double thread for the cable and single for the interlacing.

1

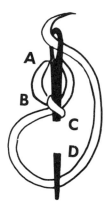

Work a Chain Stitch, coming up at A and going down again at A, holding the loop open – come up inside this loop at B and draw flat.

2

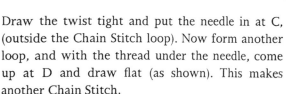

Holding the needle as shown, twist the thread once around it (as in French Knots).

3

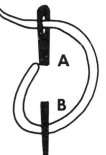

Draw the twist tight and put the needle in at C, (outside the Chain Stitch loop). Now form another loop, and with the thread under the needle, come up at D and draw flat (as shown). This makes another Chain Stitch.

4

Repeat #2 again and continue making a Chain Stitch and a French Knot alternately so that the finished effect is like the diagram.

5

Using a blunt needle and a contrasting colored thread, lace the "cables" together (as shown). Do not draw the interlacing thread too tight.

Whipped Stem Stitch

Whipped Stem Stitch makes a fine smooth line stitch when the Stem Stitch is whipped with the same color. (The Stem Stitches should not be too long). An attractive candy cane effect is obtained if a contrasting color is used for the whipping. Generally it is best to use double thread in this case.

1

First work a line of Stem Stitch. (*See diagram – "Stem Stitch".*)

2

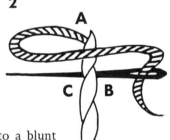

Then coming up at A change to a blunt tapestry needle and go through from B to C where stem stitches overlap one another. Pass only under the stitches, not through the material.

3

Continue, by repeating #2, until the whole line is whipped – finished effect should be like a raised cord.

Pekinese Stitch

This is a decorative stitch best worked as a single line, several close together are difficult to do. Keep the first back stitching small and even, and do not leave the loops too long. The finished result should be like a neat braided edging.

Work a line of Back Stitch, coming up at A and going down at B, into the same hole as the previous stitch (as shown).

1

B A

2

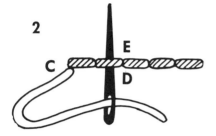

With a contrasting color, using a blunt needle, come up at C (just below the first Back Stitch). Slide the needle upwards through the second Back Stitch (not through material), from D to E (as shown). Leave a loop.

3

Then slide downwards through the first Back Stitch from F to G. Bring the needle out on top of loop made by the first stitch; pull flat, but not too taut.

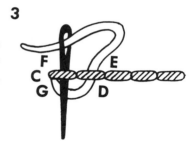

4

Now slide the needle upwards through the third Back Stitch from H to J; leave a loop as in #2.

Slide the needle downwards through the second Back Stitch from E to D, as in #3. Bring needle out on top of loop made by the previous stitch; draw flat.

5

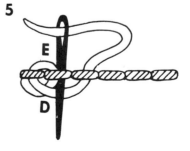

Repeat #2, 3, 4, 5, making a row of interlacing stitches into the Back Stitches. The low edge has a series of even loops, while the upper edge is flat (as shown).

Backstitched Chain Stitch

138

1

Work a row of ordinary Chain Stitch. Then with a contrasting color, Back-stitch through it, coming up in the center of one Chain Stitch and going down in the center of the one before.

2

Finished effect. This stitch is equally effective when used as a solid filling with several rows side by side.

Threaded Back Stitch

Work a line of Back Stitch, and using a blunt needle and contrasting color, thread it through as shown. The needle passes under the first Back Stitch from right to left (not into the material), through the second Back Stitch from left to right, and so on. Do not draw the interlacing thread too tightly or the effect will be lost.

Interlaced Running Stitch

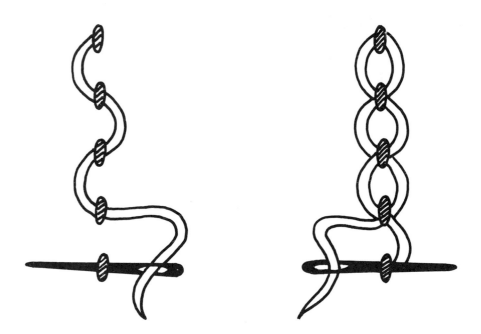

With a heavy thread work a row of Running Stitches, then with a blunt needle and contrasting color, thread it through as in Threaded Back Stitch. Finally thread it back in the other direction, to make ovals of equal tension, as shown.

Interlaced Herringbone Stitch

First work a row of Herringbone. Beginning on the right, with a blunt needle and contrasting thread pick up the first bar of the Herringbone, slanting the needle downwards. Pick up the next bar slanting the needle upwards (direction of needle is indicated by arrows). Continue to the end of the line.

Threaded Herringbone Stitch

First work a row of Herringbone. With a blunt needle and contrasting color, pick up the under thread of the Herringbone cross, and weave along first the upper, then the lower edge in this way, as shown.

Tied Herringbone Stitch

First work a line of plain Herringbone. With a blunt needle and contrasting thread, slide the needle under the Herringbone cross, pointing the needle towards the center of the line. While needle is held in position, twist thread over and under the needle, as shown. Draw tight to knot it. Work this Coral Knot on each cross along the line, always pointing the needle toward the center of the Herringbone band.

So called because each one is a small separate entity, which may be used either as a "powdering" lightly scattered to fill an area, or solidly, close together, or simply as a single isolated stitch.

Raised Spider's Webs

Raised Spider's Webs should be small and may be either whipped or woven.

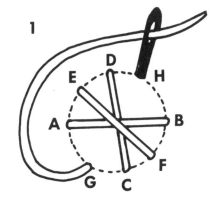

Using a blunt (tapestry) needle, come up at A, down at B, across center of circle.

Then come up at C, and down at D, (C to D should be slightly off center as shown.) Come up at E down at F, up at G, and down at H. (H goes in quite close to D.)

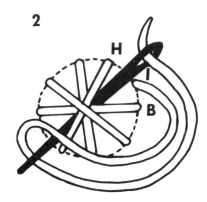

This leaves a space for the needle to come up finally at I, a point midway between H and B. Then slide the needle under all the threads at their intersection. Take the thread and loop it across the needle and then under it as shown. Draw through and pull upwards to knot threads together in center.

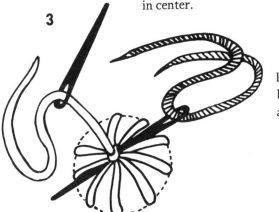

Pulling the knotting thread upwards, take another blunt needle threaded with any contrasting color and push it under all the spokes.

Unthread this needle and pull upwards with both strands of this contrasting thread, so that all the spokes are taut (as shown). Continue to hold it upwards while weaving round and round as in ordinary Woven Spider's Webs. Push in enough rows of this weaving so that the spider's web stands up in a point. Finally pull out the contrasting working thread, leaving the spider's web firmly raised.

Bullion Knots

Double thread is usually best for this stitch. The knots may be used individually, or worked side by side. They should not be too long, or they will curl instead of lying flat on the material.

Bring needle up at A, go down at B, but do not pull thread through.

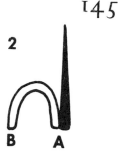

Stab needle up at A again but bring it only *halfway* through material.

Holding needle from below, twist thread round needle at A, until number of twists equals the distance between A and B.

Holding top of needle and threads firmly with finger and thumb of left hand, draw needle through with right hand, loosening coil of threads with left hand as you do so, to allow needle to pass through freely.

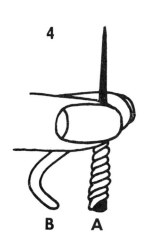

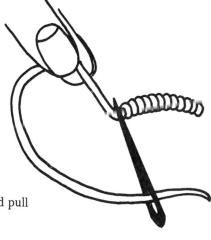

Then place needle against end of twist, at the same time pulling on the thread, as shown, until the knot lies flat on the material. If any "bumps" appear in the knot, flatten these by stroking the underneath of twist with the needle, at the same time pulling on the thread.

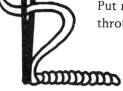

Put needle in close, at the end of the twist and pull through firmly.

Raised Needle Weaving

This is a good companion to Bullion Knots, but it has a slightly broader effect. It looks more attractive as a detached petal if it tapers at either end. Take care to draw the weaving thread very tight at both ends in order to bring this about.

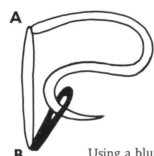

Using a blunt needle, come up at A, go down at B, and repeat, coming up at A, down at B again, so that two stitches lie side by side. Do not draw too tight.

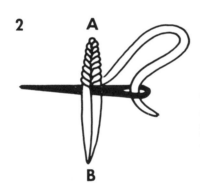

Coming up at A once more, start to weave, (without going through the material). First pick up the left hand thread, pushing the needle through from right to left.

Then pick up the right hand thread, pushing the needle through from left to right. Continue till the two underlying threads are completely covered. From time to time pack the weaving threads together by pushing them up with the needle. Keep the tension even so that the line will be smooth.

French Knots may be scattered like seeding, to fill an area lightly, or they may be arranged in rows to fill a space solidly. The latter is most effective if each row is clearly defined and the knots lie evenly side by side. Alternatively they may be sprinkled closely but unevenly to produce an intentionally rough surface.

1

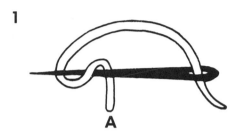

Bring needle up at A, twist thread once round needle as shown.

2

Put needle in at A, or just beside it, pull the thread until it fits *closely* round the needle (not too tightly). Pull needle through.

3

The finished knot. The thread should only be twisted once round the needle, as this makes a neat knot; *never* two or three times. The size of the knot is determined by the number of threads and size of the needle used.

Detached Chain Stitch

Make a single Chain Stitch and anchor it down with a small stitch (as at the end of a row of Chain Stitch). This stitch may be used as a filling, combined with cross bars, or scattered over the ground as a "powdering" like seeding.

Detached Twisted Chain

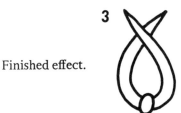

Come up at A, go down at B level with and to the left of A. Holding the thread across and then under the needle as shown, come up at C, in the center below A-B.

Anchor the stitch down outside the loop at D.

Finished effect.

Index of Stitches

Acknowledgments

Page 2 Courtesy, Victoria and Albert Museum. Crown Copyright

    3 Designed by the author. Worked by Mrs. Eugene Geddes. Photograph by Hans Van Nes Studio

    6 By kind permission of the Trustees of Victoria and Albert Museum, London. Photograph by John R. Freeman & Co., London

  11 Courtesy, Victoria and Albert Museum. Crown Copyright

  15 Courtesy, The Folger Shakespeare Library, Washington, D. C.

  17 Courtesy, Victoria and Albert Museum. Crown Copyright

  19 *Left:* Courtesy, Victoria and Albert Museum. Crown Copyright. *Right:* Courtesy, Museum of Fine Arts, Boston

  20 *Top:* Courtesy, The Cooper Union Museum. *Bottom:* Courtesy, Museum of Fine Arts, Boston

  21 Courtesy, Museum of Fine Arts, Boston

  22 Courtesy, Museum of Fine Arts, Boston

  24 Courtesy, Museum of Fine Arts, Boston

  25 Courtesy, Museum of Fine Arts, Boston

  26 By kind permission of the Trustees of Victoria and Albert Museum. London. Photograph by John R. Freeman & Co., London

  32 Photograph by Hans Van Nes Studio

  33 Designed and worked by the author. Photograph by John R. Freeman & Co., London

  35 Worked by Mary G. Grayer. Photograph by John R. Freeman & Co., London

  40 Designed by the author. Worked by Mrs. Grover O'Neill. Photograph by Hans Van Nes Studio

  51 Courtesy, Museum of Fine Arts, Boston

  53 Designed by the author. Worked by Mrs. John B. Marsh. Photograph by Hans Van Nes Studio

  54 Designed by the author. Worked by Mrs. Randall J. LeBoeuf, Jr. Photograph by Hans Van Nes Studio

  55 Adapted by the author from a design in the Shelburne Museum. Worked by Mrs. Barent Lefferts. Photograph by Hans Van Nes Studio

  56 Adapted by the author from an embroidery in the Victoria and Albert Museum. Worked by Mrs. Thomas J. Watson. Photograph by Chris Corpus

  58 Designed by the author. Worked by Mrs. F. C. Windisch. Photograph by Hans Van Nes Studio

59 *Top*: Designed by the author. Worked by Mrs. William F. LaPorte, Jr. *Bottom*: Designed by the author. Worked by Mrs. John B. Marsh. Both photographs by Hans Van Nes Studio

60 Designed and worked by the author. Photograph by Hans Van Nes Studio

62 Designs from patterns in the Victoria and Albert Museum, London

63 Courtesy, Victoria and Albert Museum. Crown Copyright

64 Designed by the author. Worked by Mrs. Hermann G. Place. Photograph by Hans Van Nes Studio

65 Designed by the author. Worked by Mrs. William Mitchell Van Winkle, Jr. Photograph by Chris Corpus

66 Courtesy, Victoria and Albert Museum. Crown Copyright

67 Courtesy, Victoria and Albert Museum. Crown Copyright

68 Designed by the author. Worked by Mrs. Donald Bush. Photograph by Hans Van Nes Studio

69 *Top*: Designed by the author. Worked by Mrs. Hampton S. Lynch. *Bottom*: Designed by the author. Worked by Mrs. Norman P. Clement, Jr. Both photographs by Hans Van Nes Studio

70 Courtesy, Victoria and Albert Museum. Crown Copyright

71 Courtesy, Victoria and Albert Museum. Crown Copyright

74 Designed by the author. Worked by Mrs. Barent Lefferts. Photograph by Chris Corpus

75 *Left*: Designed by the author. Worked by Miss Louise E. Opitz. *Right*: Designed by the author. Worked by Mrs. E. Farrar Bateson. Photographs by Hans Van Nes Studio

79 Courtesy, Victoria and Albert Museum. Crown Copyright. Photograph by John R. Freeman & Co., London

80 *Top right* and *bottom left*: Courtesy, Victoria and Albert Museum. Crown Copyright

81 Courtesy Royal School of Needlework, London. Worked by the author. Photograph by Hans Van Nes Studio

93 Courtesy, The Metropolitan Museum of Art, Rogers Fund, 1922

104 Worked by the author. Courtesy, Royal School of Needlework, London. Photograph by Hans Van Nes Studio

119 Courtesy, Victoria and Albert Museum. Crown Copyright. Photograph by John R. Freeman & Co., London

134 Designed and worked by the author. Photograph by Chris Corpus.

141 Courtesy, Victoria and Albert Museum. Crown Copyright. Photograph by John R. Freeman & Co., London

Facing Page 12

Curtains

from Longfellow's Wayside Inn, Sudbury, Massachusetts. Designed by the author from an embroidery in the Cooper Union Museum. Worked by Mrs. Edwin C. Jameson, Mrs. Hermann G. Place, Mrs. Harry Peters and Mrs. Barent Lefferts. Kodachrome by Vladimir Kagan.

Mirror

Adapted for embroidery by the author from a painting by Mrs. Charles Platt. Worked by Mrs. John B. Marsh. Kodachrome by Hans Van Nes Studio

Facing Page 27

Bulman bed and detail

Old Gaol Museum, York, Maine. Kodachrome by Vladimir Kagan

Facing Page 32

Vest

Designed and worked by the author. Kodachrome by Hans Van Nes Studio

Cushions

Designed by the author. *Top left :* Worked by Miss Elizabeth Riley, adapted from a design in the Cooper Union Museum. *Top right :* Worked by Mrs. Donald Bush. *Bottom left :* Worked by Mrs. William F. Lamb. *Bottom right :* Worked by Mr. Stephen Christy. Kodachrome by Chris Corpus

Facing Page 50

Wing chair

Worked by Mrs. Hermann G. Place

French chair

Worked by Mrs. Thomas J. Watson

Both designed by the author. Both kodachromes by Chris Corpus

Facing Page 66

Design for a cushion

Designed and worked by the author. Kodachrome by Hans Van Nes Studio

Facing Page 70

Owl

Designed and worked by Mimi Housepian. Kodachrome by Roland Rojas

Jacket design: Designed by the author. Worked by Mrs. Randall J. LeBoeuf, Jr.